The 1970s Sports Moped phenomenon

Funky Mopeds!

Richard Skelton

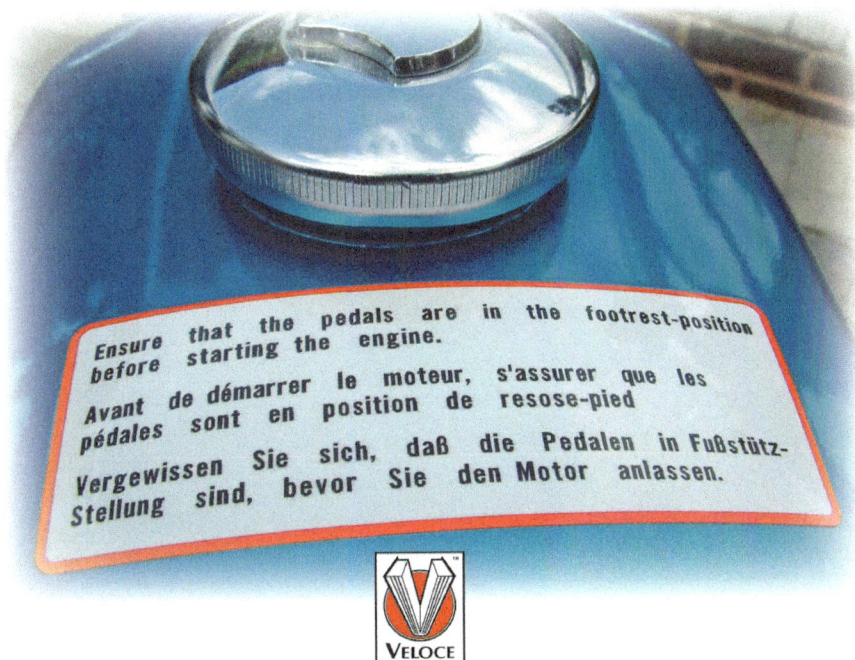

VELOCE PUBLISHING
THE PUBLISHER OF FINE AUTOMOTIVE BOOKS

For post publication news, updates and amendments relating to this book please visit: www.veloce.co.uk/books/V4078

www.veloce.co.uk

First published in 2004 by Veloce Publishing Limited, Veloce House, Parkway Farm Business Park, Middle Farm Way, Poundbury, Dorchester, Dorset, DT1 3AR, England. Fax 01305 250479/e-mail info@veloce.co.uk/web www.veloce.co.uk or www.velocebooks.com.
Reprinted April 2006, February 2013 and May 2016.
ISBN: 978-1-845840-78-5 UPC: 6-36847-04078-9.

© Richard Skelton and Veloce Publishing 2004, 2006, 2013 and May 2016. All rights reserved. With the exception of quoting brief passages for the purpose of review, no part of this publication may be recorded, reproduced or transmitted by any means, including photocopying, without the written permission of Veloce Publishing Ltd. Throughout this book logos, model names and designations, etc, have been used for the purposes of identification, illustration and decoration. Such names are the property of the trademark holder as this is in no sense an official publication.
Readers with ideas for automotive books, or books on other transport or related hobby subjects, are invited to write to the editorial director of Veloce Publishing at the above address.
British Library Cataloguing in Publication Data – A catalogue record for this book is available from the British Library. Typesetting, design and page make-up all by Veloce Publishing Ltd on Apple Mac. Printed by CPI Group (UK) Ltd, Croydon, CR0 4YY.

CONTENTS

Acknowledgements 4

Introduction 5

**Chapter one: A brief history
   of the sports moped** 8

Chapter two: Moped people 16
Barry Moore 16
Brent Fielder 17
Charlie Owens 17
Chris Alty 18
Chris Mahon 18
Gerry Croxson 19
John Dunn 19
John Powell 20
Mark Wilson 20
Neil Holland and Julian Kowalewski 21
Paul Simcox 23
Peter Padgett 24
Russell and Margaret Marsden 25
Russell Sears 25
Steve Fitzsimmons 25
Steve Wilkinson 26
Terry Silvester 27

Chapter three: That was then 28
Boom! 28
Getting it together 30
Which moped? 30
Garelli 31
Honda 31
Yamaha 32
Fantic 32
Gilera 32
Puch 33
Casal 33
Gitane 34
Taking to the road 34
Pack culture 35
Sixteen and stupid! 37
Police 39
Speed 39
Tuning 40
Pros and cons 41
Maintenance and reliability 42
Pedals 43
Cool dudes 45
Training and tests 46
What happened when we were 17? 46

Chapter four: ... and this is now 47
Pure nostalgia 47
Restoring, collecting, and riding 49
Finding bikes and parts 52
Hard earned skills 59
Partners 59
Letting go 61
The Sports Moped Owners' Club 61
Moped runs 63

Mk I and Mk II Garelli Tiger Crosses. A landmark model in the sports moped story.

The fabulous Fantic Chopper was fast and handled surprisingly well.

Funky Mopeds

Barry Moore's restoration checklist	67
Chapter five: Gallery	70
Chapter six: The fabulous FS1-E	88
FS1-E chronology	90
L Reg (1 August 1972 to 31 July 1973)	90
M Reg (1 August 1973 to 31 July 1974)	90
N Reg (1 August 1974 to 31 July 1975)	91
P Reg (1 August 1975 to 31 July 1976)	91
R Reg (1 August 1976 to 31 July 1977)	91
S Reg (1 August 1977 to 31 July 1978)	91
Fizzy Galore	93
The FS1-E on ebay	94
www.fs1e.co.uk	95
Chapter seven: Slopeds	96
Chapter eight: 1970s sports mopeds	100
AJW	100
Batavus	101
Casal	102
Cimatti	103
Derbi	105
Fantic Motor	105
Flandria	109
Garelli	110
Gilera	114
Gitane	115
Honda	117
Kreidler	118
KTM	119
Malaguti	121
Motobecane	124
Negrini	124
NVT	124
Puch	124
Suzuki	128
Testi	130
Yamaha	130
Zundapp	133
Who do you think you are, Barry Sheene?	134
Number one hit singles in the sports moped era	135
500cc World road racing champions	137
That was the year that was	138
Index	141

ACKNOWLEDGEMENTS

The author (left) and school friend Andrew Bishop on their N- registration purple FS1-Es in 1977. Note the FS1-E DX bolt on downtubes on Andrew's bike. (Courtesy Andrew Bishop)

I would like to thank the following people for their help and co-operation, over the many months it has taken me to put this book together. Firstly, all the 'moped people,' and in no particular order, Paul Simcox, Barry Moore, Chris Alty, John Powell, Russell Sears, Charlie Owens, John Dunn, Gerry Croxson, Steve Wilkinson, Chris Mahon, Neil Holland and Julian Kowalewski, Mark Wilson, Russell and Margaret Marsden, Peter Padgett, Terry Silvester, Brent Fielder, and Steve Fitzsimmons.

Other people who have helped me include Andy Betts, Dave Clark, Paul Clark, Andy Bishop, Ian Ritchie and Matt Chambers.

I am also grateful to Rod Grainger at Veloce Publishing for taking on the project. Finally, I would like to thank my dad for buying me my Yamaha FS1-E back in 1976, and getting me started in motorcycling.

Richard Skelton

INTRODUCTION

On 15 December 1971, Tory Transport Minister, John Peyton, changed British two-wheeler licensing regulations, and unwittingly created a market for a new breed of machines, which were produced by manufacturers from all over the world.

The infamous 'sixteener law' wiped all 16-year-old motorcyclists off the road in an instant, forcing them to turn to mopeds. The law was intended to force novice bikers onto their grannies' 50cc shopping bikes, or off the road altogether, thereby reducing accident statistics at a stroke.

The Gitane Comfort VI Automatic – the sort of moped the Government had in mind for sixteeners.

The Government's plan was successful at first, but soon market forces were at work. Manufacturers and importers realised there was a demand for real motorcycles, and produced more powerful models to meet it. Equipped with pedals, added as a token gesture to comply with the law, 50cc performance motorcycles were imported to the UK in increasing numbers from 1972. The sports moped had arrived.

These sporty machines, soon dubbed 'sixteener specials', gave a first taste of freedom and independence to hundreds of thousands of teenagers. Ostensibly stopgaps for beginners itching to ride bigger bikes or learn to drive a car, these machines represented so much more to a generation of youngsters.

Bound together by the commonality of their machines, which was given away by their irrelevant and slightly embarrassing pedals, these kids made their way through their first 12 months on the road enjoying camaraderie and rivalry, impressing their mates and girlfriends, and, above all, in their own eyes, looking impossibly cool. It was a happy and carefree time for many.

Despite learning the hard way about hazards such as car drivers' blind spots, wet leaves under trees, and lorry diesel on roundabouts, it was a relatively safe motorcycling baptism. Most sports mopeds were hard pushed to exceed 50mph, which was nonetheless fast enough to keep up with town traffic, unlike the wobbly, slow step-through models the Government had wanted teenagers to ride. On top of this they had efficient brakes, and excellent handling and stability.

Stylish 'sixteener specials' flooded into the UK from around the world. Moped roadsters, trail bikes, motocross bikes, cafe racers, and even choppers found their way onto the market, making the moped sector the largest sales category in motorcycling.

As ever, all good things come to an end. From 1 August 1977, a new legal definition of moped came into force, obliging manufacturers to warrant that their 50cc machines' "maximum speed in still air, and on level ground carrying a rider weighing 75kg (11st 11lb) does not exceed 30mph by more than five mph." Pedals were no longer necessary, and there was also an absurd maximum weight limit of 250kg.

The manufacturers responded with power restricted versions of their current models, and by producing attractive new designs meeting the new regulations, but to no avail. The moped was back in the gutter, and a huge drop in 50cc registrations helped boot motorcycle sales into the doldrums, bringing an end to the 1970s motorcycle boom.

Soon the supply of second-hand sports mopeds ran out, and around ten years after it began, the sports moped era fizzled out.

Thrashed, crashed, and ill-maintained by a succession of 16-year-olds, most sixteener specials ended up being scrapped or further abused as field bikes before eventually being left to rot away. However, a handful lying neglected in garages, sheds and barns survived into the 1990s, and started to become sought after by collectors and restorers.

Now the sports moped revival movement is in full swing, and many models have attained classic status.

An increasing number of enthusiasts are actively resurrecting, and preserving these rare machines. There is a network of spares outlets and suppliers, and a lively owners'

Funky Mopeds

What it was all about - bicycle pedals added to 50cc motorcycles. Note Fantic's prancing pony design, cheekily echoing Ferrari's famous logo.

club. There are displays of concours restorations at classic motorcycle shows; a website devoted to the most popular model, historic registers have been drawn up, runs are held all over the country, and a museum is being planned. To quote collector Eamonn Maloney: *"It's men behaving sadly I suppose."*

This book celebrates the phenomenon of the sports moped. It charts the history of the genre, and attempts to recapture the spirit and times of the 1970s seen through the eyes of a sixteener. In the book there is an illustrated guide to the many manufacturers, with colour photographs of the key models and many obscure examples are also depicted - if you have owned a sports moped, your bike will probably be in here somewhere!

This book also looks at the current bike scene, and includes stories of restorers and collectors - men enjoying owning again the bikes they rode when they were sixteen. Some ride their mopeds for fun, some use them sparingly on club runs and rallies, and others keep their lovingly restored machines in pristine, unused condition, bringing them out only for display at shows and exhibitions.

Although the merits and shortcomings of various makes and models are reviewed and discussed, this book is not primarily intended as a technical publication. Use it to open

Introduction

a door to the past. Journey back through a haze of two-stroke exhaust smoke to the 1970s world of Slade, Barry Sheene, and cheesecloth shirts. To a time when the Laverda Jota and Kawasaki Z1 were kings of the road. When reps drove Mark III Cortinas, and parents all over the country were coerced by their 16-year-old offspring into letting them take to the road on 'sixteener specials' ...

Early examples of the Yamaha FS1-E. The archetypal sports moped.

www.veloce.co.uk
Details of all Veloce books • New book news • Special offers • Newsletter

CHAPTER ONE

A BRIEF HISTORY OF THE SPORTS MOPED

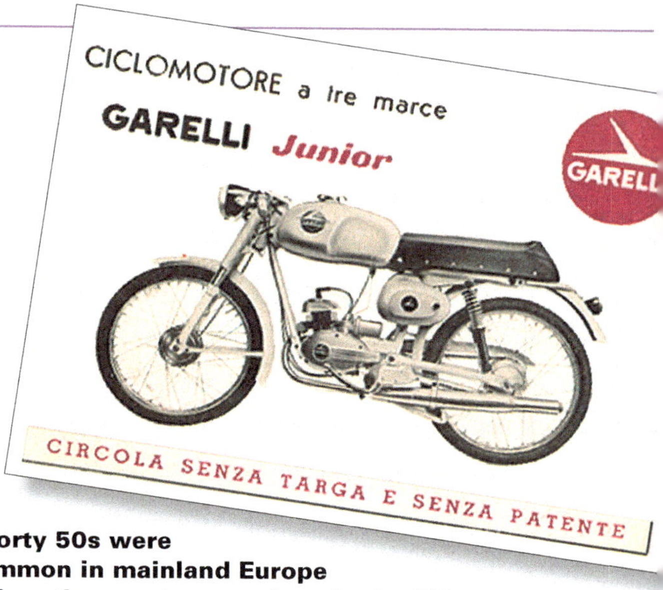
CICLOMOTORE a tre marce
GARELLI Junior
CIRCOLA SENZA TARGA E SENZA PATENTE

Sporty 50s were common in mainland Europe before the sports moped era in the UK.

Our story starts at the beginning of 1972. *'Ernie - The Fastest Milkman In The West'* by Benny Hill was being knocked off the top of the UK pop charts by the New Seekers hit, *'I'd Like To Teach The World to Sing'*, inspired by the Coca Cola ad, and 16-year-old would-be motorcyclists began the new year cursing Ted Heath's Conservative Government for taking their wheels from under them.

Until December 1971,16-year-olds could ride bikes of up to 250cc, and the announcement of the new law by the Transport Minister, John Peyton, brought a howl of protest from the British motorcycle fraternity. Motorcyclists then, as now, were paranoid about motorcycle legislation from the Ministry of Transport, seeing it as deliberately anti-biker, and designed to deter young people from taking to two wheels at all.

Passions ran high in the motorcycle press. The gist of the argument against the new regulations was that novice bikers would be far less vulnerable keeping up with traffic on machines with enough acceleration to get out of trouble, or overtake a tractor on a country lane, than crawling along in the gutter, bobbing in the wake of trucks and buses.

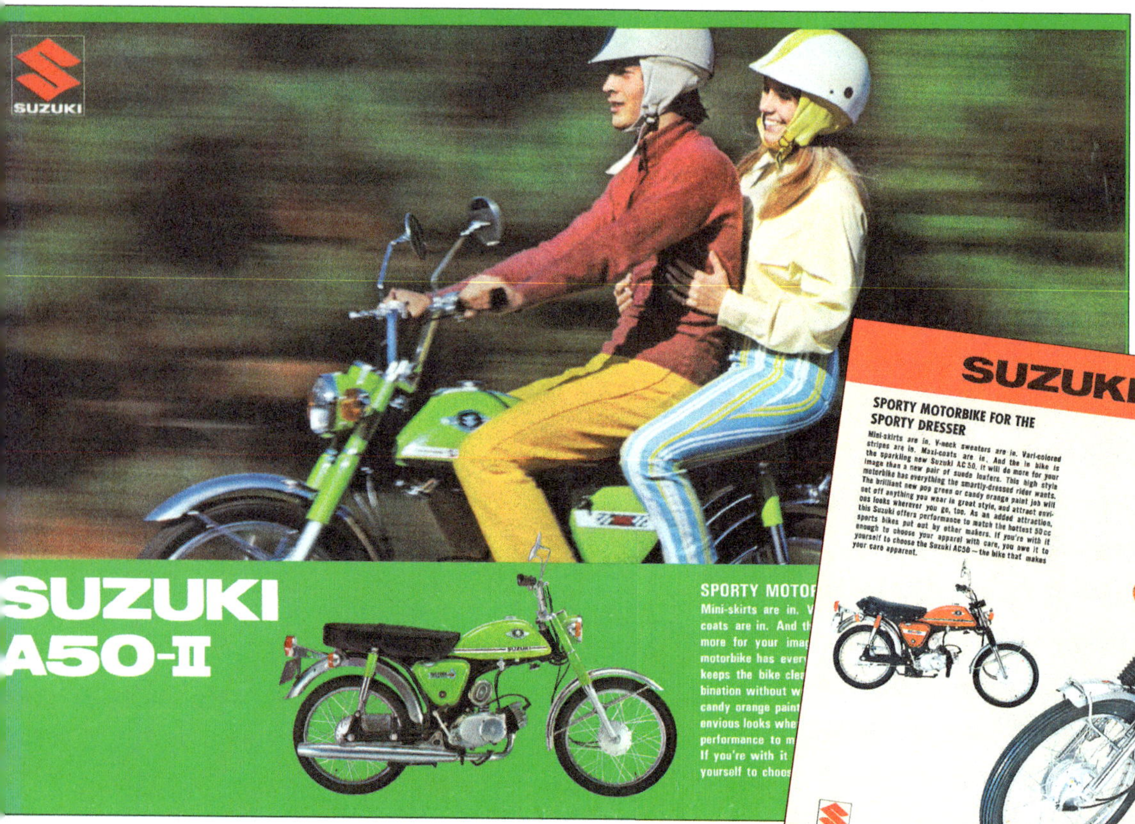
SUZUKI
SUZUKI
A50-II

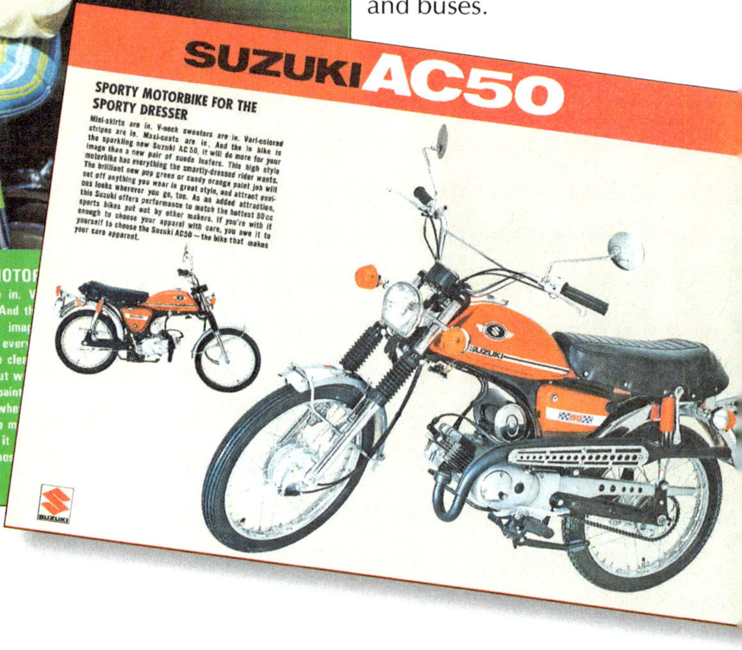
SUZUKI AC50
SPORTY MOTORBIKE FOR THE SPORTY DRESSER

Suzuki's 50cc motorcycles formed the basis of its AP50 sports moped.

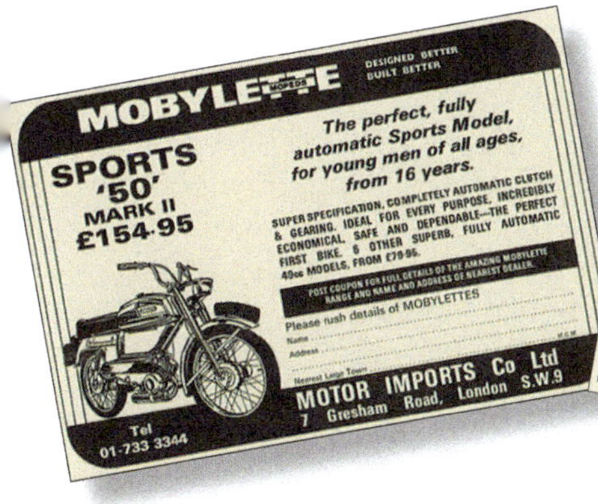
MOBYLETTE
MOPEDS
DESIGNED BETTER
BUILT BETTER
SPORTS
'50'
MARK II
£154·95
The perfect, fully automatic Sports Model, for young men of all ages, from 16 years.
SUPER SPECIFICATION, COMPLETELY AUTOMATIC CLUTCH & GEARING. IDEAL FOR EVERY PURPOSE. INCREDIBLY ECONOMICAL, SAFE AND DEPENDABLE—THE PERFECT FIRST BIKE. 6 OTHER SUPERB, FULLY AUTOMATIC 49cc MODELS, FROM £79·95.
POST COUPON FOR FULL DETAILS OF THE AMAZING MOBYLETTE RANGE AND NAME AND ADDRESS OF NEAREST DEALER.
Please rush details of MOBYLETTES
Name
Address
Nearest Large Town
MOTOR IMPORTS Co Ltd
7 Gresham Road, London S.W.9
Tel
01-733 3344

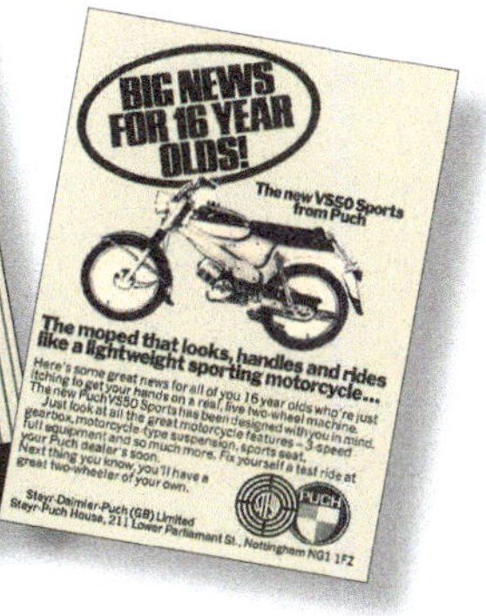
BIG NEWS FOR 16 YEAR OLDS!
The new VS50 Sports from Puch
The moped that looks, handles and rides like a lightweight sporting motorcycle...
Here's some great news for all of you 16 year olds who're just itching to get your hands on a real, live two-wheel machine. The new Puch VS50 Sports has been designed with you in mind. Just look at all the great motorcycle features – 3-speed gearbox, motorcycle-type suspension, sports seat, full equipment and so much more. Fix yourself a test ride at your Puch dealer's soon. Next thing you know, you'll have a great two-wheeler of your own.
PUCH
Steyr-Daimler-Puch (GB) Limited
Steyr-Puch House, 211 Lower Parliament St., Nottingham NG1 1FZ

Big news for 16-year-olds: sports mopeds are coming!

The definition of a moped in the UK, at that time, was 'a two-wheeler of less than 50cc and equipped with pedals which must be able to drive the machine.' Typified by the ubiquitous Puch Maxi, the mopeds of the day were slow devices, with single or automatic gears, developed from pedal cycles and cyclemotors (bicycles with an engine attached to either front or rear wheel).

Popular throughout the world, particularly at times of economic strife, mopeds were first created by adding a light engine to a conventional bicycle. The earliest motorcycles can also claim to be mopeds as pedals were necessary to aid their poor performance on hills. The late 1940s saw the first

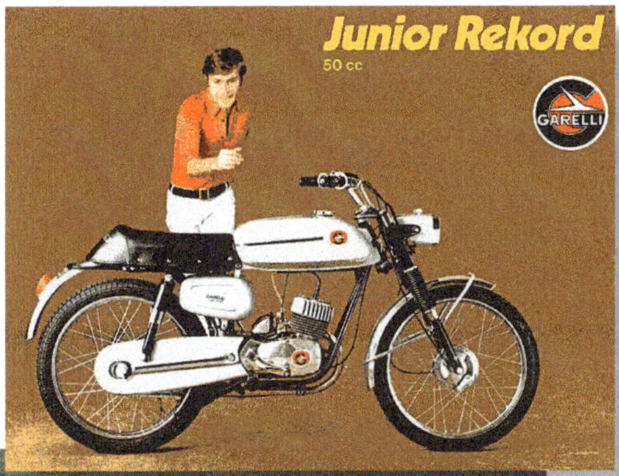
Junior Rekord
50 cc
GARELLI

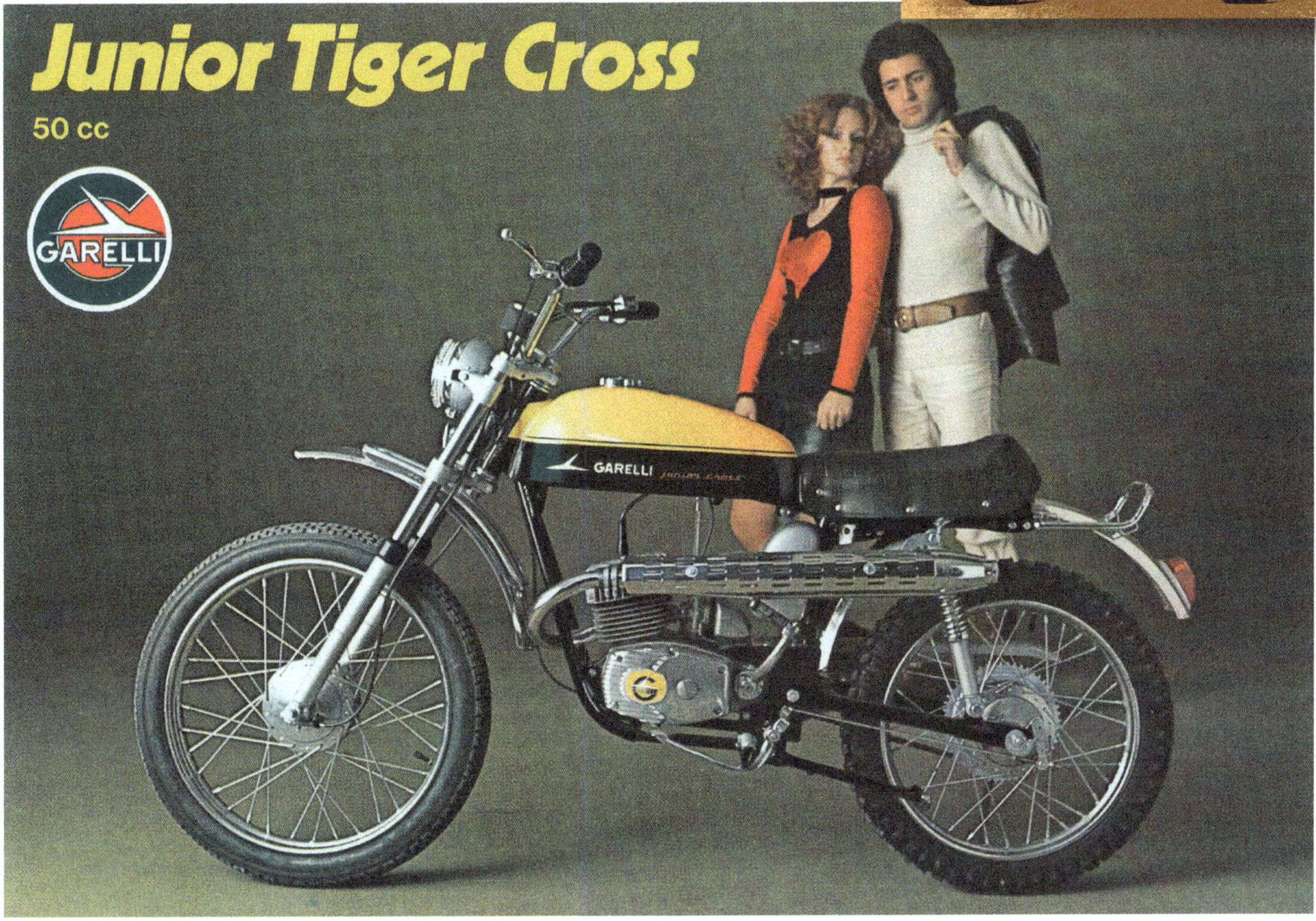
Junior Tiger Cross
50 cc
GARELLI
GARELLI

Garelli upped the stakes by adapting its Rekord and Tiger Cross models for the UK market.

Funky Mopeds

machines with small engines, which transmitted power via a roller onto a tyre. In the 1950s, models with stronger frames, proper suspension, and hub brakes were produced. The moped became ubiquitous in many European countries with a range of styles developing, including pseudo-racers as well as runarounds.

Mopeds made up only a small percentage of UK two-wheeler registrations, and were not considered part of the proper motorcycling scene. Models on sale in Britain offered dismal performance, and had comic, almost ironic names such as Norman Nippy, Phillips Gadabout, and Raleigh Runabout.

There was no tradition of moped riding in the UK, unlike France and most of mainland Europe. There, then and now, 14-year-olds could ride these machines on the road without taking any sort of test. Another feature of their small bike scene was the presence of ultra-lightweight motorcycles, often using tuned moped engines. These were usually quite sporty in nature, had footpegs instead of pedals, and were ridden by teenagers and adults alike. This type of performance moped screamed around at 50mph or even 60mph, unlike the more prevalent step-through models, which could manage only half that speed.

It was these European machines, sometimes specially adapted to incorporate pedal mechanisms, that led the way in circumventing the new British licensing legislation. The Japanese manufacturers, which had their own lightweight motorcycles suitable for conversion, were soon to follow.

By the summer of 1972, there were early signs of a response to the sixteener law from motorcycle manufacturers and the British bike trade. *Motorcycle Mechanics* magazine tested a selection of mopeds, two of which, the Motobecane Sports 50 Mk II and the Puch VS50, had been designed to look something like motorcycles, and offered reasonable (35-40mph) performance. A Puch advertisement for the VS50 promised youngsters 'the experience of motorcycling' on their 50cc machine, and the historic Italian Gilera firm announced new models in the pipeline that certainly looked considerably more exciting than shopping mopeds. Garelli was also arriving on the scene, and Fantic Motor, Casal, and Yamaha did too before the end of the year.

Puch's VS50 was smartly turned out in yellow and chrome. It had a three-speed twistgrip gearchange, telescopic forks, and swinging-arm rear suspension, and was capable of speeds over 35mph. It was available in the UK from March 1972, and prompted *Motorcycle Mechanics'* tester to announce *"The Puch VS50 sports moped is probably the nearest machine to a motorcycle that any 16-year-old enthusiast can legally ride on the roads."*

However, Puch's trailblazing effort was pitched too conservatively, and was soon overtaken by the opposition. Three months later, Garelli, from Como in Italy, began exporting a moped version of its established 50cc motorcycle, the Rekord, and an exciting off-road style model, the Tiger Cross. These machines boasted 6.5bhp, had four-speed foot change gearboxes, and a top speed of around 57mph. By Christmas, Fantic had begun shipping its sensational chopper moped and the sporty little TI (*Tourismo Internazionale*), which had a similar specification to the Garelli. At the same time, Yamaha was bringing in the first UK 'sixteener special' versions of its 50cc FS1. The first SS-badged FS1-Es (E for England) were sold in January 1973, and were a spectacular overnight success.

That January, *Motorcycle Mechanics'* editor, Charles E Deane wrote *"A new generation of sports moped is coming onto the market. Whether it is right that 55-60mph mopeds should be allowed is debatable, but the Ministry of Transport made the regulations, and you can't blame manufacturers for finding ways to combat them."* He then mused about the

Sports mopeds flooded into Britain from around the world.

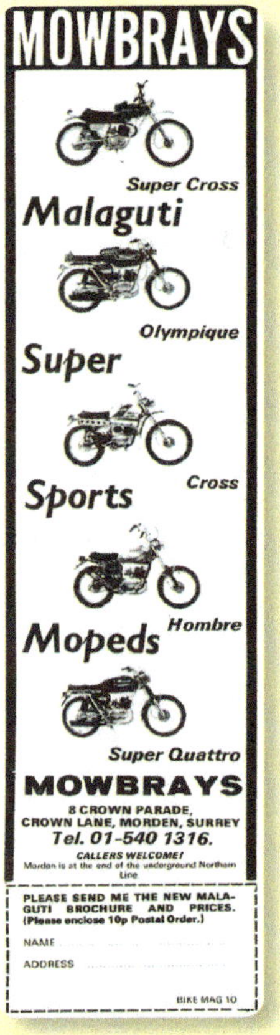
MOWBRAYS
Super Cross
Malaguti
Olympique
Super
Cross
Sports
Hombre
Mopeds
Super Quattro
MOWBRAYS
8 CROWN PARADE,
CROWN LANE, MORDEN, SURREY
Tel. 01-540 1316.
CALLERS WELCOME!
Morden is at the end of the underground Northern Line
PLEASE SEND ME THE NEW MALAGUTI BROCHURE AND PRICES.
(Please enclose 10p Postal Order.)
NAME
ADDRESS
BIKE MAG 10

The 1975 Malaguti sports moped range.

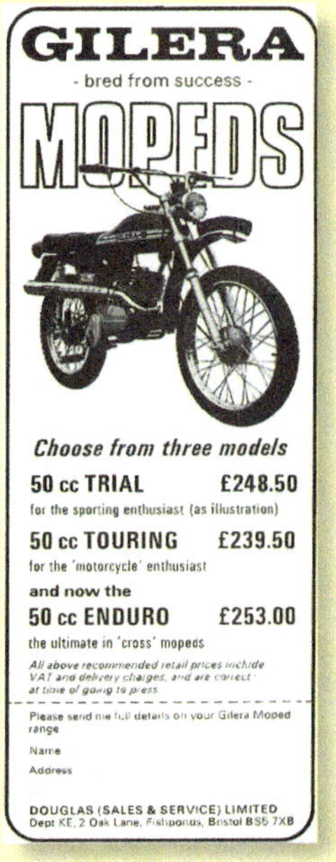
GILERA
- bred from success -
MOPEDS
Choose from three models
50 cc TRIAL £248.50
for the sporting enthusiast (as illustration)
50 cc TOURING £239.50
for the 'motorcycle' enthusiast
and now the
50 cc ENDURO £253.00
the ultimate in 'cross' mopeds
All above recommended retail prices include VAT and delivery charges, and are correct at time of going to press
Please send me full details on your Gilera Moped range
Name
Address
DOUGLAS (SALES & SERVICE) LIMITED
Dept KE, 2 Oak Lane, Fishponds, Bristol BS5 7XB

By 1974 there were three sports moped models in the Gilera range.

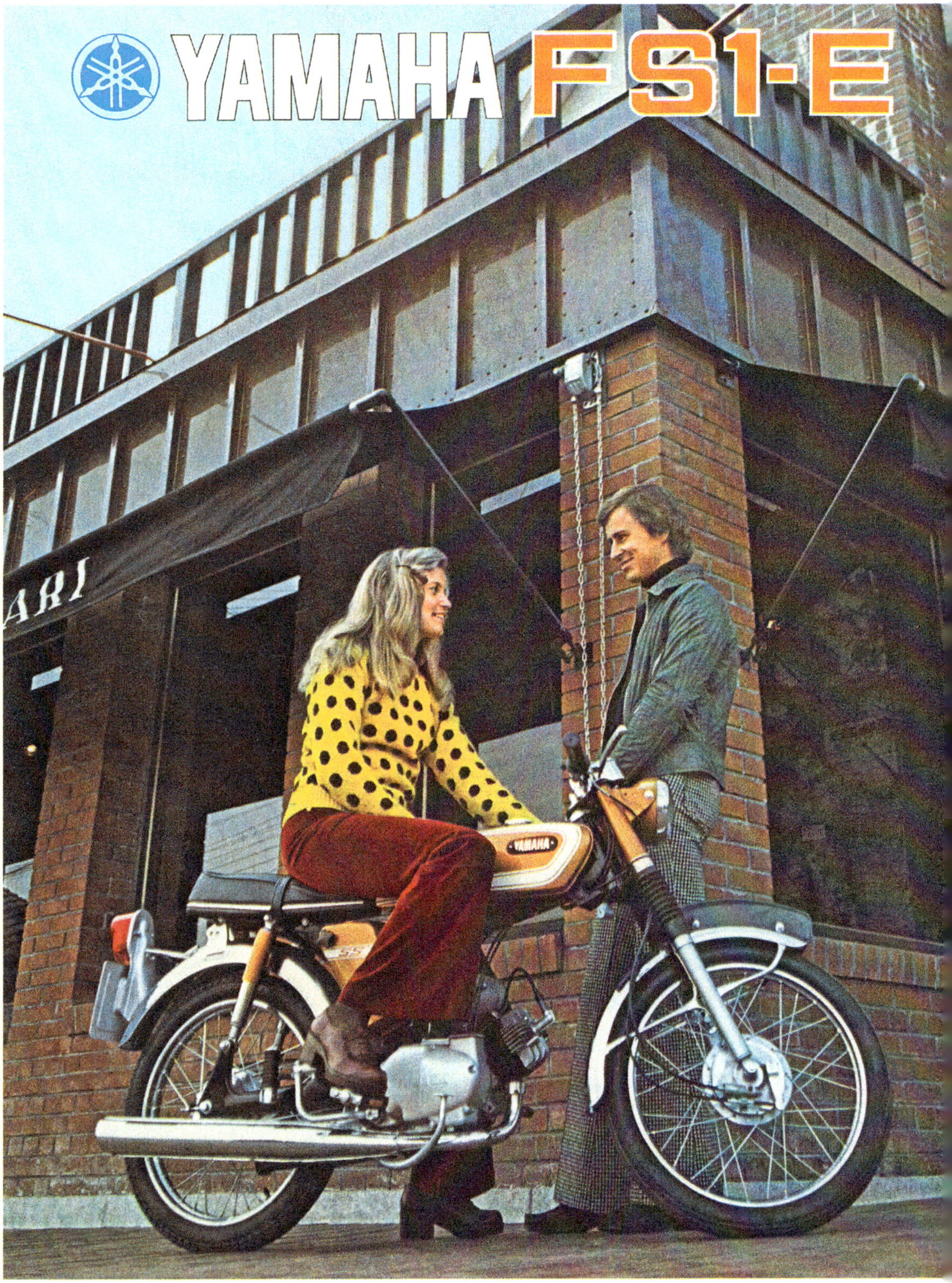
YAMAHA FS1-E

Legendary Grand Prix racer Jarno Saarinen and his wife Soili were recruited to help advertise the new Yamaha FS1-E. Tragically, Saarinen was killed in the 1973 Italian 250cc Grand Prix at Monza the following year.

Funky Mopeds

At the end of the sports moped era, there were nearly 50 models to choose from.

possibility of converting 110mph racing 50s for road use, and fitting them with pedals to *"... really make a monkey out of Peyton, and his sixteener ban."*

However, not all motorcyclists had been totally against the new laws, and many in the trade were beginning to see that the Peyton legislation was having a positive, rather than negative, effect on motorcycling. Yorkshire Yamaha dealer and former 60s TV scrambling star, Terry Silvester does not agree the sixteener legislation was designed to be anti-biking. He said –

"The new law was simply designed to stop 16-year-olds getting on bikes that were too fast for them, but the Government had NSU Quickly-type machines in mind. When the sports models came in, it got mopeds away from the step-through stigma, and created an affordable, and appealing way into motorcycling, which ultimately did the trade a favour."

A brief history of the sports moped

The Testi Champion Special. Things were getting extreme at the top end of the market.

For a number of reasons, explored later in this book, the newly created sixteener moped scene not only offered a sensible starting point for young motorcyclists, it actually encouraged thousands to take to two wheels, who wouldn't otherwise have done so. Its attraction hooked many of them into becoming lifelong bikers.

The floodgates opened, and over the next five years sports mopeds were to become commonplace on British roads. This made mopeds the most overcrowded sales classification in British motorcycling, with over 50 different models available to the public during this period. Moped registrations helped to kick-start the mid-seventies motorcycle sales boom, which later saw 272,261 two-wheel registrations in 1976, and 265,513 in 1977.

Popular European sports mopeds included Italian Fantics, Gileras, Garellis, and Malagutis, Austrian Puchs, and Portuguese Casals. Of the 'big four' Japanese manufacturers only Kawasaki stayed out of the market. Generally speaking, the Italian and other European machines were faster and more exotic, and the Japanese models offered better reliability and build quality. The British bike industry, in its last decade as a major force in world motorcycling, failed to recognise a golden opportunity to win over young customers, responding only belatedly with the oddball NVT Easy Rider ER4TL.

There was, and is, a great deal of debate about just how fast the many different sports mopeds were, and the issue was clouded by the inflated claims of riders and manufacturers. But one thing is certain - novice bikers in the seventies were definitely able to travel a great deal faster on these machines than the Government had foreseen, or intended.

Terry Silvester said *"The Yamaha FS1-E had a top speed in the forties, which was just right, but the Italians got in on the job and pushed the envelope right out of the top. Their 60-65mph bikes were too fast, and the Government had to do something."*

Accidents involving 16-year-olds had reduced dramatically in 1972. On the face of it this seemed to indicate the Government had got its thinking right, but it was arguably a result of there being far fewer people of this age group on the road, rather than mopeds being inherently safe.

From the following year, however, the converse was true. Because of the increasing number of moped registrations, accident statistics soared. Under 50cc machines were involved in 40 per cent more accidents in 1974 than 1973, and, inevitably, the legislators' attention once more focused on the sixteener category.

As early as the summer of 1974, *Bike* magazine predicted the possibility that *"some killjoy Government minister might decide that mopeds capable of over 50mph are far too hazardous for the repressed youth of today."*

The Government was indeed keen to act, and new legislation was already being drafted to redefine the moped. Rumours began to circulate of a 28mph blanket speed limit with new regulations to force sixteeners onto step-through type machines. As a damage limitation strategy, importers and manufacturers talked of a voluntary 40mph restriction, and the industry proposed training as the answer to rising accident statistics.

The motorcycle press again resented the changes, quoting the same arguments about the relative safety of brisker, more competent machines, but resistance was more muted this time. Meanwhile a wave of anti-motorcycling hysteria, targeting sports mopeds in particular, built to a peak in 1976.

Three infamous anti-moped reports that year embodied everything objectionable about tabloid-style journalism; they were sensationalist, exaggerated, one-sided, sloppily researched, and selectively written.

The cover story in the January/February edition of the AA's *Drive* magazine made an astonishing attack on sports mopeds by highlighting a crash by a young rider. According to this piece, the rider's injuries were *"the result of a crash on a moped of a type that safety experts call a death trap in the hands of novices."*

The feature took up seven pages, but gave no detail of the accident central to the story. A motorcycle magazine editor of the time, incensed at the slipshod nature of the article, tracked down and spoke to the rider, discovering he had ridden off the road on his Yamaha FS1-E and hit a tree at low speed, as a result of looking behind for too long. The only damage to the bike was a bent pedal and a broken indicator lens.

There was more sensationalism on BBC's *Nationwide* on 5 May. Picking up the moped-bashing baton, it contrived a report focused on reporter Richard Stillgoe, a non-motorcyclist, riding an FS1-E at Brands Hatch.

He announced *"I've never been on one of these things before, and I've just been around Brands Hatch at 50-60mph. It was terrifying."* Describing the bike as a *"killer"* he added it could be *"ridden at any speed"* and *"looked like*

Funky Mopeds

a high powered motorbike." The report ended with a drag race towards Paddock Hill Bend between the Yamaha and a commuter moped, which was pedalled off the line.

Then in October, *The Guardian* reported forthcoming new moped legislation, in sensationalist fashion, on its front page. Under the heading *"Brake on Boys' 80mph Machines"* the story reported *"high speed mini-motorcycles dressed up as racing machines, and giving engine notes like hysterical wasps, on which so many 16-year-olds have buzzed to their deaths."*

The piece also contained the line *"Motorcycle technology has advanced so rapidly that manufacturers, particularly the Japanese, have been able to drag out undreampt of power from 50cc engines."*

Undreampt of power? As statistics elsewhere in this book show, the Japanese constructors were among the most cautious and responsible of the sports moped manufacturers. Although 100mph plus performance from 50cc competition engines had been commonplace for many years, mid-70s Japanese sports mopeds struggled to exceed 50mph downhill.

Throughout early 1976, behind the scenes meetings were taking place between Government officials and industry representatives, concerning forthcoming new moped legislation. Some concessions were secured as a result. Motorcycle-style frame geometry was retained, and pedals ceased to be a legal requirement, but a 40mph speed limit was never going to be acceptable to the politicians. A compromise was reached with a 30mph design speed, with 5mph leeway, giving an effective absolute maximum speed of 35mph. There were no plans to adopt the common European practice of allowing 14-year-olds to ride 20mph step-throughs.

The new regulations were announced in the summer of 1976 and finalised by the end of the year, but the Government insisted on 1 August 1977 as the implementation date. Old-style sports mopeds would continue to be legal provided they were first registered before this date, so this gave dealers and importers time to build stockpiles of R plates, ahead of the ban - and they did. A total of 25,752 'sixteener special' machines were registered in July 1977 compared with 7576 the year before.

Stocks soon ran out, and the new "slopeds" began to appear on the roads. They still looked sporty, but were painfully slow, as were sales. The sports moped had been emasculated, and it was the beginning of the end for the genre and the culture that had grown up around it.

Modifications to restrict the power of current models were fairly straightforward, and there were a number of articles in the motorcycle press reviewing performance kits, and detailing the changes necessary to derestrict new machines.

Changing carburettors and inlet manifolds would often release a great deal more power. Other models were stifled by their air filters or exhaust pipes, or held back by tiny gearbox sprockets. The February 1978 issue of *Motorcycle Mechanics* magazine reviewed a £27 kit, which added 18.5mph to the top speed of a Fantic Caballero. Throttle response and breathing was also reported as greatly improved.

Motorcycle dealers remember turning down sixteeners' requests to make their post 1977 mopeds go faster, and no doubt some of the new machines were modified, but many riders, and their parents, were either too concerned about invalidating their insurance to take the risk, or feared a dramatic increase in performance would likely draw the attention of the police. Tuning for more speed had been part of the moped scene for many years, but it had never been illegal to tamper with a moped's performance in this way.

Existing sports mopeds became scruffy and worn out as years of thrashes, crashes, ham fisted maintenance, and general lack of care in the hands of a succession of 16-year-old owners took its toll. The sports moped was becoming increasingly rare on British roads, and was passing into motorcycling history. Without an attractive starting point at 16, a whole generation of motorcyclists was lost. Not interested in "slopeds" or semi-wrecked old sports mopeds, many took to cars at 17 without

A brief history of the sports moped

ever experiencing life on two wheels.

Accident figures did drop as a result of the new legislation, but that was probably due more to the fall in the number of sixteeners on the road. It had been argued for some time that excess speed was not the primary cause of most motorcycle accidents. In fact, it was typical that the Government had chosen to ignore a report from the Transport and Road Research Laboratory in 1974, which indicated that four out of five motorcycle accidents occurred at 30mph or less.

The 1977 moped law (actually amendments to the Motor Vehicles (construction and use) Regulations 1973) was the first performance legislation for private vehicles. More was to come, of course. The performance gap between the new mopeds and 250cc machines was vast, and the revised moped law insisted that machines up to 150cc must carry identification plates, which paved the way for a lower learner age limit for motorcycles.

In 1983, a long anticipated 250cc learner ban came into force, restricting 17-year-olds to 125cc machines limited to 12bhp. Motorcycle learner legislation has been tinkered around with since, several times, to make a convoluted and complicated set of rules. These seem to exist as much to make it as off-putting as possible to enter the world of motorcycling, as to reduce accidents.

Biking in Britain is currently enjoying another boom, which is being fuelled in part by a return to two wheels of many of the sports moped generation. The 1971 sixteener law may go down in history as the only motorcycle legislation which actually served to boost biking, bringing joy to thousands of teenagers in the process ...

The pressed steel framed Puch VS50 was, arguably, the first purpose-built sports moped. (Courtesy Nick Waite)

CHAPTER TWO

MOPED PEOPLE

The individuals profiled in this chapter were all involved in the 1970s sports moped scene. As well as contributing to the research for this book, their comments and views are quoted throughout the text.

BARRY MOORE

An incredible 141 sports mopeds have passed through Barry Moore's hands since he started restoring them back in 1996. Now he has only two machines in his collection, and he's open to offers on one of those!

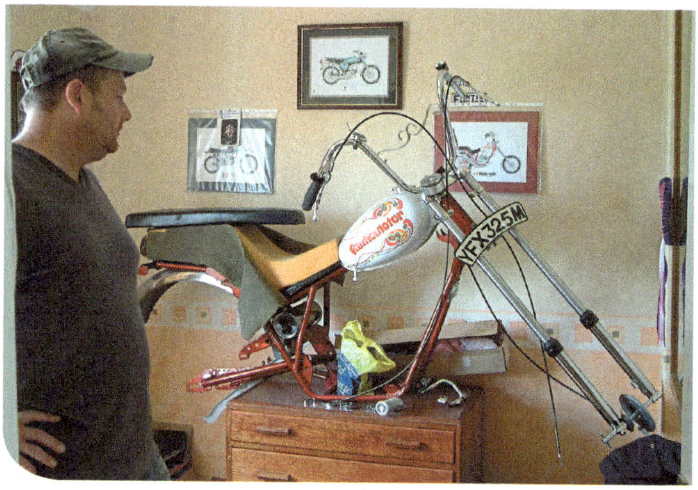
YFX325M

Barry Moore.

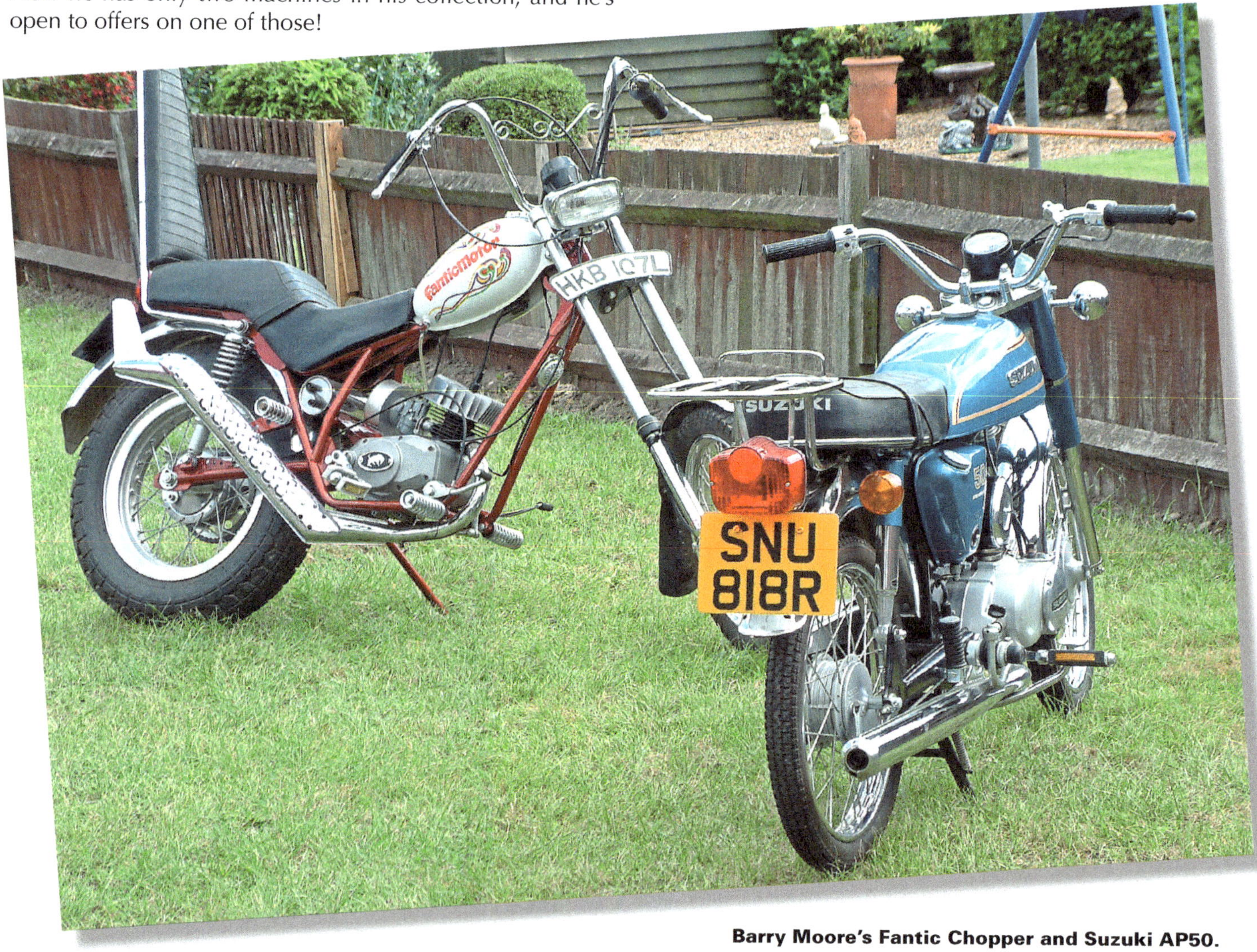
HKB 107L
SNU
818R
SUZUKI

Barry Moore's Fantic Chopper and Suzuki AP50.

Moped people

For Barry, the pleasure is in restoring and riding, rather than owning the bikes, and he enjoys the wheeling and dealing as well.

It all started when he read about a barn-find Suzuki AP50 in a classic motorcycle magazine. *"I thought 'Wow!', I was inspired, and I went straight out and bought the* Evening Post *and* Loot.*"* Immediately, Barry found an AP50 for sale in Northamptonshire, and negotiated to buy it for £65. He brought it back home to Nottinghamshire in the back of his Ford Fiesta XR2. Barry said *"I got it home, stripped it and restored it the best I could. Then I MoT'd it, and sold it for £450."*

Barry's next move was to put a wanted advert in his local free advertiser. This yielded another AP50, a rusty Yamaha FS1-E, and then triggered an avalanche. *"Before I knew it, I had nine FS1-Es and a Yamaha TY50P in the cellar; then I filled the shed up. My first proper restoration was a gold SS FS1-E that was used in a* Shredded Wheat *television advert. Next, I did the TY50P."*

Working with official parts books, these early bikes were correct down to the nuts, washers, and original tyres. *"When I'd done a few I knew where I could cut corners if I really needed to, but some bikes have to be 'bob on'."* Next, Barry turned his attention to a yellow and blue Gilera Touring then a Cimatti Kaiman.

For the next few months, Barry travelled the region collecting rusted mopeds to restore. At weekends, he ventured further afield to shops and autojumbles in search of spares. *"I'd buy everything they'd got. I took out what I wanted and sold the rest, so a lot of my bikes didn't owe me very much."*

By now, it had become an obsession. *"At one point I had 36 'peds. They were stacked in the garage, I had eight in the shed, four in a brick outbuilding, five in the attic, and four or five in the cellar. I stuffed them everywhere I could - and she still hasn't left me!"*

Although times are quieter now, Barry is keen to carry on. *"I'm sure there are 'peds to be found though I wouldn't fancy doing an FS1-E now, some of the parts are just too hard to find."*

"I like messing around with cars, but I'll always have bikes. I love restoring them. Then there's the chasing bit, tracking down bikes and spares, getting the last elusive part, finishing them, and getting them running again. Then I can sit back and say, 'I've done that, that's another one brought back to life'."

He's not sentimental about his restorations. *"People nag me to sell, they go on at me until eventually, I cave in. My Cimatti was rare and fast, and people said, 'Why did you sell that?'. But you've got to sell, to buy another, to get restoring again. And if you ride them as I do they go downhill. They're not made to last forever, are they?"*

The two bikes Barry has kept are a Suzuki AP50, and a Fantic Chopper. *"The AP50 means a lot to me because it's the bike I had when I was 16, but if I could be 16 again, I'd have a Fantic. It's the noise they make, I would love another Super T even now."*

Another one?

Barry did find a Super T a few years ago, but inevitably, he let it go. He said *"I swapped it for a Malaguti Monte before I knew how rare Super Ts are."*

Almost as rare as a Super T, Barry's Fantic Chopper is for sale to the right person, at the right price. But this time it's not a mistake. In the spare bedroom, half finished, a mint replacement is taking shape.

BRENT FIELDER

Brent Fielder, a Garelli enthusiast, is a self-taught restorer, and a hardcore member of the Sports Moped Owners' Club.

He is one of the earliest sports mopedists, having first taken to the road in 1973, not long after the Peyton legislation came into force.

Brent is an active rider, and a wry, and intelligent observer of the sports moped scene. He writes about these things both expertly and amusingly in his *Brent's Bit* column in the bi-monthly SMOC newsletter.

Brent is now a senior statesman among the seventies sixteener fraternity, and it's not only for reasons of chronology that he holds that position. Although modest about his achievements, Brent is a more than competent mechanic and restorer, who runs a small fleet of vintage and classic motorcycles.

CHARLIE OWENS

Charlie Owens, from the Peak District in Derbyshire, is a much respected restorer of classic Japanese motorcycles. He has been a 'fizzy' fan since he bought his first one for £30 in 1977, at the age of 14.

Charlie now has several exotic Italian superbikes, and he's kept some beautiful, multi-award-winning classic Kawasakis he has restored. It's his fizzy, though, that he would find most difficult to part with if he had to reduce his collection.

Fanatical beyond belief, Charlie made sure that when he restored his orange and purple FS1-Es, even out of sight bolts and washers were totally authentic by using parts from broken Yamahas of the same model year, shipped in from the USA. His sports mopeds also stand out from other restorations by the original paint on their tanks and other tinware.

The FS1-Es have won a number of prizes at classic shows, but even now he's not satisfied. *"There are still some touches I'd like to do, I'm always looking for improvement."* he said.

Funky Mopeds

Charlie Owens has won many awards with his 1973 FS1-E.

Charlie aged 16.

Charlie had several jobs after leaving school, eventually settling down to build up a successful skip hire company. However, by the late 1990s, restoring bikes was taking up more and more of his time. Eventually, he sold the skip business, and bought a job lot of more than a thousand accident damaged bikes from the USA. He then set up working full time as Seventies Classics.

As well as his FS1-Es and bigger bikes, Charlie has rebuilt a Triumph Stag to concours condition, and he's also a keen restorer of Raleigh Choppers. "Everybody wants what they had, or dreamed of having when they were a kid, don't they?"

CHRIS ALTY

Chris Alty, secretary of the Sports Moped Owners' Club, has been a fan of small motorcycles since taking to the road, on

Chris in action on his Kreidler racing bike. (Courtesy Chris Alty)

a Honda SS50, towards the end of the sports moped era in 1978.

A founder member of SMOC, Chris runs the club and edits its bi-monthly newsletter along with his wife, Paula. In recent years he has been a regular competitor in 50cc races on a pair of Kreidlers with exotic ex-Grand Prix engines.

"I like the underdog, and getting the most out of the least," said Chris. "You don't need a great big bike to go fast. If the bike's right, and you ride it hard, you don't need a large capacity machine. I've beaten 250s in mixed class races, and you should see their faces."

CHRIS MAHON

Chris Mahon, a Fantic fanatic, was entrepreneurial as a 16-year-old, dealing in Fantic motor spares to fund running his own Super T. He was still ahead of his time, nearly 20 years later, as a groundbreaker in the early days of the sports moped revival movement.

Chris got the biking bug early after having a lift on his uncle's scooter, at just eight years of age. "That sowed the seed," he said. "I was only ten, or eleven, when I bought my first bike, a Mobylette, for 20 Embassy cigarettes, the summer after leaving junior school. After that I had lots of field bikes, which I rode at our own scrambles track - James, Francis Barnetts, Villiers, and a Suzuki K10, a fantastic little bike.

"I was very independent," he continued "My parents thought it was better I was on bikes, than on the streets. Then I found I had mechanical aptitude, and could fix them and

Moped people

keep them running. By the time I was 16, I was dealing in Fantic spares as a sideline."

By this time, Chris was on the road, having bought his older brother's Fantic Super T. He developed a great affection for the Milan marque that stayed with him through the 1980s, when he had a number of bigger bikes. Then in 1992, he came across a Super T frame, and developed an urge to build a bike around it.

After teaming up with Gary, a fellow enthusiast, Chris scoured the country for bikes and spares, intending to get the Super T together and go on to collect, or build, the whole Fantic range. Chris and Gary attended the inaugural sports moped run and photoshoot, which was instigated by *Classic Motorcycle Mechanics* magazine in 1995, then hosted the meeting in Swindon in 1996 that led to the formation of the Sports Moped Owners' Club.

Chris did collect the full Fantic range, and he continued to ride bigger road bikes regularly until a bad accident a few years ago. The resulting ill health prevented him from maintaining his bikes properly, let alone riding them. Now, sadly, the collection is deteriorating a little, but Chris retains his passion for Fantics, and his encyclopaedic knowledge of all things Fantic remains very much intact.

GERRY CROXSON

Gerry Croxson and I went to the same school. We were in the same class, and he celebrated his sixteenth birthday three days after I did, in November 1976. I had a second-hand purple Yamaha FS1-E (XAN 92N if anyone's seen it lately), and Gerry took to the road on a red Gilera Touring.

Gerry's Gilera. (Courtesy Gerry Croxson)

Although Gerry was not typical of the sixteener generation, he did represent a significant minority. His sports moped was bought purely as a means of getting to work, and he had no passion for, nor interest in, bikes before he turned 16.

Nevertheless, he enjoyed his first year of powered transport so much that he went on to become a bike fan, riding on into the 1980s. Gerry and I lost touch in the early 80s after I moved away, resuming contact as we neared 40.

No longer involved in the motorcycling scene in any way, Gerry would nonetheless like to get back on a bike at some point. When he does it might not be a sports moped, but it will probably be a classic 70s motorcycle of some sort.

Gerry was part of the 1976-77 sports moped scene in and around the village of Flackwell Heath, near High Wycombe in Buckinghamshire, and so was I. It was the strong and happy memories of those days that led eventually to me writing this book.

The line-up of kids and 'peds from Pembroke Secondary School, Spring Lane, Flackwell Heath in our academic year was as follows:

Shaun Allen (Malaguti Monte)
Andy Betts (Suzuki AP50)
Andy Bishop (Yamaha FS1-E)
Dave Clark (Honda SS50 4 speed)
Gerry Croxson (Gilera Touring)
Mark Davies (Malaguti Monte)
Glen Douglas (Yamaha FS1-E)
Mark Dubois (Gilera Enduro)
Peter Mitchell (Honda SS50 ZB2)
Daras Rich (Honda SS50 4 speed)
Richard Skelton (Yamaha FS1-E)

Apologies to anyone I've missed out.

JOHN DUNN

John Dunn adapted the skills he had honed as a successful restorer of classic performance cars to transform a dilapidated wreck of a Puch Grand Prix Special into a show-stopping prize winner.

Incapacitated by a massive traffic accident in 1992, John was unable to manage the heavy work involved in rebuilding the Mark One Escort twin-cams and Mexicos he had specialised in refurbishing. So he turned instead to his first vehicular love, sports mopeds.

As a 16-year-old, John had ridden home-tuned Yamaha FS1-Es and a Puch M50 Sport. He became a great admirer of the Austrian firm's classy Grand Prix Special model after spotting one of the rare machines in a neighbouring Nottinghamshire village. Many years later, while recovering from his accident, he saw a rough one at an autojumble and had to have it. His uncle ran a bike breaking business, and John was surprised to find there the actual bike he had admired as a teenager. He salvaged some parts from it, then set about finding

Funky Mopeds

more spares to rebuild the autojumble find. He eventually completed the restoration to a very high specification, after finding some rare items in the possession of a long retired Devon Puch dealer.

In a number of ways, the bike is better finished than the original, and John makes no apologies for this. *"I try to achieve the best results possible, and the bike is pretty authentic, but if I can make some improvements to its performance and appearance along the way then that's fine,"* he said.

John's dad was a biker, and a vintage car enthusiast, and John received some help getting started as a mechanic. Most of his skills he has learned by taking things apart and finding out how they work. John likes working with mopeds because he enjoys the challenge of making their tiny engines produce extra power, but he is also a fan of genuinely fast machinery. As well as tuning his FS1-E, and modifying the Puch, John has enjoyed extracting extra performance from motocross bikes, racing karts, and a number of ultra-fast cars and motorcycles over the years.

JOHN POWELL

When John Powell was a teenager in the 1970s, he dreamed of owning a Kawasaki Z1B or a Rickman Z1000, but it was the well-used gold SS FS1-E, which got him on the road for

John Powell and his FS1-E. The first of many. (Courtesy John Powell)

the first time, that now symbolises biking happiness for this motorcycling fanatic.

John is a big fan of 1970s aircooled two-stroke twin cylinder Yamahas (he owned 10 at the last count), and he rides modern superbikes too, but it's for the humble fizzy that he has a special affection.

Together with his mate, Steve, from Poole, John has spent thousands of hours restoring FS1-Es and tracking down spares. Between the pair of them there's not much they don't know about the archetypal sports moped. They travel the country going to autojumbles, sleeping overnight in their van to be able to pick up bargains early in the morning, and they regularly attend Sports Moped Owners' Club rallies across the UK.

Having just moved house, John has made a big effort to scale down his FS1-E collection from its peak of ten machines, but new bikes keep turning up. When a bike is sold a new project takes its place.

John was, until recently, a teacher in a girls' grammar school, and he persuaded the authorities to let his pupils rebuild FS1-Es for him in their motor vehicle studies lessons. *"I just didn't get the time,"* said John. *"And the girls loved it!"*

MARK WILSON

Reminiscing in the pub on a Saturday night led Cumbrian Mark Wilson to be reunited with the sports moped he rode when he was sixteen.

Gitane Champion Veloces are rare machines, and it had

Mark Wilson with his beautifully restored Gitane Champion Veloce.

Moped people

been many years since Mark had last seen one on the road or even in a magazine. On bumping into a former biker friend at a town centre bar, it turned out he had Mark's actual bike in his shed, and it had stood there for more than twenty years.

Mark said *"My brother had run the bike for a while after me, but he'd seized it, and parts were hard to obtain, even then. My brother gave it to this friend who'd stripped it down, but that's as far as he got. The friend then asked me when my brother was going to pick up the bike."*

Mark went round the next day. The bike was all there, and he *"gathered it up and fetched it home."* Not having done any serious restoration before, he got onto the internet to begin his research. After a short time, he came across Chris Alty, secretary of the Sports Mopeds Owners Club who has since become a good friend. *"The club is run by good people who will do anything they can to help,"* said Mark, who has made a number of vital contacts through the SMOC.

Mark soon became very knowledgeable about Gitanes, and he received a call from someone in Oxford asking for advice. *"I helped him the best I could."* said Mark, *"Then he rang back a week later and asked if I wanted to buy his bike. We haggled for two weeks by e-mail before I met him at the Newark autojumble, and bought it for £200."*

The second Gitane had also spent more than 20 years in a shed, and had sustained serious front end damage at some time in its life. It was very original, and almost all there, so Mark decided to restore the Oxford bike first.

Less than eight months later, the moped had been restored to the highest standards and was attracting admiring crowds on the SMOC stand, at the Stafford classic bike show.

Mark has now turned his attention to his own machine. He said *"I've found good people now, people to do welding, plating, paint, and graphics. This will make the next one easier, but there's still plenty of hard work ahead. There's no substitute for elbow grease, and it pays to clean up everything the best you can."*

A successful teenage motocrosser, Mark continued to compete as an adult, and has always prepared his own bikes. *"I've always been mechanically minded, and I've always had bikes, so I do the engines and wheels myself."*

When the second Gitane is completed, Mark's got a Testi lined up to restore as a runabout and for moped runs. Another Champion Veloce, this time from Edinburgh, sits at the side of the garage. Mark is going to be around the sports moped scene for some time to come.

NEIL HOLLAND AND JULIAN KOWALEWSKI

Julian Kowalewski was a little apprehensive when Neil Holland turned up on his doorstep in the early 1990s. Neil had been a bit of a hard nut when they had been at school together, but

Neil Holland.

Julian needn't have worried; the two were about to become firm friends due to their shared passion for sports mopeds, especially Garellis.

Neil was already interested in restoring sports mopeds, and knew Julian had just bought a Garelli Rekord. He called round to see just what he planned to do with it, and found that his old school colleague was a kindred spirit.

In fact, they got on so famously they decided to team up to find more bikes to bring back to life. *"We bounced off each other well so we decided to work together."* said Neil. *"We put adverts in local papers and bike shops, and bought everything we could get our hands on."*

The pair scoured their home county of Herefordshire, and beyond, and turned up a number of finds. This included a blue Rekord MkI rolling chassis, complete with its number plate, they dragged out of a barn, and bought for £25. *"The trick is to follow up any lead or contact, whatsoever,"* said Neil.

Now a prize-winning restoration, Julian's orange Fantic TI was found in a skip *"It had been thrown away, but as soon as I asked if I could have it, it was suddenly worth money."* remembered Julian, *"I was offered it for £70, but I negotiated the price down to £30 in the end."*

Funky Mopeds

Julian Kowalewski.

In 1995, they went to the Stafford Classic Motorcycle Show, and met up with SMOC founder member, Paul Simcox. "Julian and I went to the Stafford show, and saw what was probably the first SMOC stand." said Neil. "We'd seen Paul Simcox, and the boys, in a feature in Classic Motorcycle Mechanics magazine, and it had boosted our enthusiasm even more. When we got back, we bought some parts from him, and now we're regularly in touch."

Julian and Neil's collection includes sports mopeds from a number of different manufacturers, but both rode Tiger Crosses when they were 16, and Garellis are their real passion. "The Garellis were the most attractive bikes, especially the Tiger Cross. The MkI Rekord is the fastest of the genuine sports mopeds, it feels like a 125." said Neil.

The friends ride their bikes regularly, both locally and on club runs all over the country. "Riding them adds to the satisfaction we get from restoring and owning them." said Neil, "The 70s was our era, and it brings it all back."

Moped people

Paul Simcox. Spring 1976. (Courtesy Paul Simcox)

PAUL SIMCOX

For Paul Simcox, a Midlands businessman, restoring a Garelli Tiger Cross in 1991 had life changing consequences. Paul is now at the very hub of the sports moped revival movement, with friends, and contacts, all over the world.

Paul had left mopeds behind in the 1970s, but yearned for more time on the little Italian bike that had brought him so much happiness as a 16-year-old. In 1991, he saw an advert in *Used Bike Guide* for two Tiger Crosses for sale in Crewe.

By good fortune, the seller was *"keen to swap for anything horrible and nasty,"* and Paul had a tatty, but original MZ150 Trophy in his shed. A deal was on the cards, and on April Fool's Day 1991, Paul and a mate drove up to Cheshire and came back with a bike each.

His friend decided he would just do up his, and sell it on, but for Paul the bug had bitten. The Crewe bikes were the first of many restorations he has now successfully completed, and he has helped countless other enthusiasts with advice and parts from the vast spares collection he has amassed.

Never needing to advertise for bikes or parts, Paul has built up an unrivalled network of moped contacts and sources. He has tracked down a large number of spares by finding the stored stock of long defunct bike shops.

In 1996, Paul became a founder member of the Sports Mopeds Owners Club, which was put together by a group of enthusiasts, who had come together a year earlier for a feature in *Classic Motorcycle Mechanics* magazine. The article kick-started the sports moped movement, and the club now

Paul Simcox and his Garelli Tiger Cross Mk I – the earliest known surviving Tiger Cross in the UK.

boasts over 250 members. Paul organises the club's stands at the Stafford Classic Motorcycle Shows.

He said *"Interest is growing all the time. We said at the time we're shooting ourselves in the foot, for if there's a club people will say these bikes and bits must be worth something. However, the purpose of the club is to have fun and to help people, and I think we've done that."*

During the Stafford shows, Paul has an open house, and he has hosted some memorable evenings. *"They've been some of the best nights ever, it's a great social life. It takes over your life, mine, and many other people in the club, too - in a good way."* His wife Sharon also thinks it's great *"We've met some lovely people."* she said.

Paul has a full set of Garelli mopeds comprising Rekord

Funky Mopeds

Russell and Margaret Marsden are now the owners of FS1-E spares specialists Fizzy Galore. Clockwise from left: Margaret and Margaret's brother, Malcolm. Margaret, and Russell and Malcolm. (Courtesy Russell and Margaret Marsden)

Mark I, Rekord Mark II, Tiger Cross, Tiger Special, and Rekord Cross. He also owns two Gileras, an FS1-E, a Suzuki AP50, a Malaguti Cross, and a part-restored Fantic Caballero.

Apart from the Garellis, the line-up does change from time to time: *"I occasionally sell a bike - I get an offer I can't refuse or I just run out of room. I have to ask myself, 'what aren't I going to use? What am I really interested in? Let's be practical and move on.' I was offered a silly price for my Fantic Chopper, and as I had the basis of another one in the shed, I sold it. Of course, the one in the shed is still lying there in bits."*

Unlike some moped collectors, Paul rides his bikes regularly. *"I show them at first, but then I prefer to use them. From then on, I'm not bothered about concours standards. I'm happy for them to be 95 per cent. It's no use getting caught in the rain, and having to take it apart again to clean it."*

He continued to ride big bikes in the 1990s, but hasn't had one for a while now. *"I began to realise I was having more fun at half the speed."*

PETER PADGETT

Peter Padgett has been selling bikes for more than 45 years, and the family name has become legendary in motorcycling circles because of its long-time involvement in British and World Championship road racing.

Padgett's of Batley is the longest established Yamaha dealer in Britain, and the firm has been selling the Japanese machines since the company's range caught Peter's eye, at the Earl's Court Motorcycle Show at the beginning of the sixties. *"They had new ideas, and the bikes were very impressive,"* said Peter. *"We were in on the ground floor when Japanese bikes started coming into the country, and when Yamaha's racing bikes started coming through, I started racing them myself, and my brother Don and I helped put Yamaha on the map in the UK."*

The Padgett family went on to become famous for supplying and tuning racing motorcycles, and for running racing teams at the highest levels in the sport. The racing, though, has always been underpinned by the road bike sales, and Padgett's sold hundreds of sports mopeds in the 1970s.

Peter remembers the Yamaha FS1-E with affection, and not just because he sold a great number of them. Padgett's also sold Suzuki AP50s, Honda SS50s, and Garellis.

Although his brother has retired, and his son, Clive, and other family members have been running the business alongside him for a number of years, Peter refuses to take a back seat. He remains as much an enthusiast today as he's always been.

"There's nothing like motorcycling. I keep thinking about retiring, but I'd miss it too much." said Peter. "And the bikes are better than ever. It's hard to find a motorcycle today you're not in love with." Peter still rides occasionally. "I did a lap of the TT course on a 600, a couple of years ago, in honour of Joey Dunlop. It was fantastic."

RUSSELL AND MARGARET MARSDEN

Russell and Margaret Marsden, from Huddersfield, rode Yamaha FS1-Es together in the 1970s, and now make a living running an FS1-E spares business called Fizzy Galore.

Fizzy Galore grew out of Russell's general bike breaking firm, M & M Motorcycle Spares, and now takes up most of his time. Margaret joined the business full-time in 1997, and deals with the mail order operation, as well as serving in the shop.

The couple met when Russell was 16 and riding around on a candy orange FS1-E. He spent time at Margaret's house, helping her brother Malcolm repair his crash damaged gold FS1-E, and the couple began going out together. Bitten by the biking bug, Margaret learned to ride on a Puch Maxi with help from Russell, before she too bought a fizzy, in her case an N-reg popsicle purple bike.

At that time, Russell's job was making packing cartons in a factory, but he already knew he wanted to work with motorcycles. So a year later, at 17, he had taken a pay cut to start working as a mechanic in a small motorcycle shop, earning £25 a week.

Then, in 1980, his parents helped him take advantage of a gap in the market, and he set up a bike breaking business in his home town. "My dad said 'You sell your Cortina - I got £120 for it - and I'll lend you £100.' remembered Russell, "We advertised for bikes, and used his Mini pick-up to collect them, and we found some rough old premises in William Street, in Huddersfield."

The business grew and developed, and provided Russell and Margaret with a living for nearly 20 years. The couple had no plans to diversify, but in the late 1990s, they became aware of an increase in interest in Yamaha FS1-Es. Russell said "I bought a wreck of a 1980s FS1 for £15, stripped it, and took it to the autojumble, at the BMF Show. It was a pile of rubbish, but it fetched £120. Then Margaret decided to take some pattern FS1-E mudguards to the Stafford Show and they sold well, too, so we realised something was going on out there, and pricked up our ears."

After investigating the availability of new FS1-E spares, they collected together a stock of all the genuine and pattern parts that were available. They put everything together in a catalogue, and launched Fizzy Galore, selling fizzy parts from their premises, at shows, and via mail order. It was an instant success. "It's taken over." said Russell, "The fizzy side is so busy we've run the general bike breaking side right down."

Although prepared to go back to running M & M full-time, if the fizzy boom peters out, Russell and Margaret are happier working with FS1-Es. Russell explained "It's our livelihood, but it's also about having fun because we're fizzy fans. We had good times on them, in the 70s, and we've got over 1000 customers, who did too."

RUSSELL SEARS

Russell Sears started a website for the Yamaha FS1-E, after rebuilding the wreck of the actual fizzy he rode when he was 16. His original intention was only to document the restoration, but the site quickly became the centre of the rapidly expanding 21st century FS1-E universe, attracting thousands of visits a week.

Now, due to business commitments, Russell has sold the site, but he remains a devoted fan of the fantastic fizzy, and he speaks from experience as both a restorer and member of the sports moped generation.

STEVE FITZSIMMONS

Steve Fitzsimmons, a Yorkshire car dealer, has ridden bikes ever since taking to the road on a red and black Garelli Tiger Cross, on his 16th birthday in May 1976. He has now built up a hobby restoring, collecting, and selling 1970s sports mopeds from his home.

"A few years ago, I began to get nostalgic about my moped days, and I said if I found a red and black Garelli I'd buy it." said Steve, "But I came across a yellow and black one first. I swapped a one-armed bandit and some cash for it and did it up. Then, I found a red and black wreck in Ireland, and bought it unseen for £530. It was a lot of money, but it's a rare bike."

Steve restored the Irish bike, and sold it for £2250. Then he bought a one-owner Tiger Special. "It still had its original tax disc." said Steve. "The guy ran it for six months, blew it up and left it. It had been stored for years, and there was only 3000 miles on the clock."

His new hobby gathered pace, and he began buying and restoring sports mopeds of all types. "I went all over the

Funky Mopeds

Steve Fitzsimmons and his Garelli Tiger Special, the same bike he had when he was 16.

Steve Wilkinson at home with his Gileras.

country for them. I planned to keep all of them, but now I'm getting rid of a lot. It was a challenge. You've got to beat boredom somehow. You've got to have a hobby, it keeps you out of the pub."

STEVE WILKINSON

A chance conversation with 'the missus' got Steve Wilkinson into a moped scene he didn't know existed, and, before he knew it, he became a leading authority on the Gilera marque.

An article in *Motorcycle News* about riders being reunited with their first bikes led Steve's wife, Carol, to suggest he tracked down a Gilera like the one he had when he was 16. Muttering it was impossible, and that 1974 mopeds just hadn't survived, Steve went on the internet and found one within half an hour.

It was in rough condition, and restoration didn't appeal, so he gave his details to a few moped people he discovered and left it for a while. A month later, Alan Punt, a collector, rang from Bournemouth. All his bikes were for sale including three likely Gileras.

Before long, Steve was heading south in a van with a pocketful of cash, day-dreaming of his 16-year-old self, and his yellow and blue Gilera Tourer, racing to the Wimpy drive-in with his mates in their trench coats and Stadium helmets covered in stickers.

In a moment of complete madness, Steve bought two of Alan's bikes, and returned home to add the finishing touches to their restoration. They also needed tuning and setting up; no problem for a man of 20 years' off-road racing experience.

Improving the machines, bit by bit, indulged Steve's love of working with bikes and his inquiring mind. Within a year, Steve had become a leading authority on mopeds from the Arcore factory, and has given help and advice to many Gilera restorers and purchasers.

The 1975 Gilera Trials had been lying under a hedge on a welsh farm for 20 years . It has now been restored to immaculate condition, and has been certified by the *Registro Storico Gilera* as authentic and correct in every detail.

The quality of the paint and chrome is superb, without being overdone. This is one of the few Trials restorations to be painted in the correct candy red metallic, and finished with the right white tank stripes. It also has the correct chain guard, headlamp, and Ceriani adjustable rear shock absorbers.

Steve's economy Touring model is ridden regularly, and enjoyment and practicality are more important to him than originality. He is in the process of switching the standard pressed steel, greased spring, 'pogo stick' E-type forks for oil-damped Cerianis, and he's relaxed about the frame having

Moped people

Before and after shots of Steve's 1975 Gilera Trials. Original restoration by Alan Punt.

been sprayed in the wrong silver grey.

Both machines have 6.2bhp RS engines with standard 4 speed moped gearboxes.

Steve's not one to let the grass grow under his feet - the bikes are up for sale, and he's on the lookout for a 1974 yellow and blue Touring. Anyone got a trench coat and a Stadium helmet for sale?

TERRY SILVESTER

Terry Silvester was a top TV scrambling star in the 1960s, racing against the likes of Dave Bickers, Jeff Smith, and Vic Eastwood, and in 1970 he won the Isle of Man Grand National on a 250cc Greeves.

He began his relationship with Yamaha in 1965, and in 1973, sold 40 FS1-Es from his small shop in the Yorkshire Pennine town of Holmfirth.

Terry said *"I was doing Suzukis in 1964, and was having some problems with spares so when I went to the Blackpool Show and was impressed by the Yamaha road bikes, I decided to go down that route."*

The first Yamaha models Terry sold were two-stroke twins, and although they looked impressive enough standing still, he came up with an unusual idea to sell the bikes to his customers. *"They howled like banshees,"* remembered Terry, *"so I took the first one we got up onto the road across the moor to Greenfield, and recorded the sound of it, on a reel-to-reel tape recorder, to play to people in the shop."*

Terry built up an excellent relationship with the Japanese company, and by 1973, when the FS1-E was released in the UK, Silvester's had become an established Yamaha dealership. *"It was a good little bike, and the initial sales were phenomenal."* remembered Terry, *"Yamaha was early on the sports moped scene, and the FS1-E opened up a new market."*

Although 1973 turned out to be a record sales year, Terry went on to sell hundreds more fizzies throughout the 1970s. Business became quieter at the end of the decade, then, in 1981, there was another sales boom. Terry explained *"Selling motorcycles is a funny old game, it's like riding a rollercoaster. In 1973, jobs were available for kids leaving school, and the 70s in general were a good time for us. In 1981, we got another boost, selling 150 bikes in our best year ever. Then business went down the pan in the mid-80s and early-90s. Now you can't compete unless you're big, so you've got to find a niche market."*

Finding a way to do just that, Terry wound down the road bike side of the business, and diversified into selling motocross and minibikes, and now business is booming once again. *"We may look small, but we do a lot of business,"* said Terry. *"I only sell the odd Enduro bike for the road, now. There's too much bureaucracy, and I'm glad I'm out of it."*

Silvester's still has a large Yamaha spares department, and there are still some fizzy parts on the racks. Stocks are dwindling, but Terry is happy to help if he can. He said *"People are always coming in wanting new FS1-E parts and second-hand stuff. They'll buy anything that can be straightened up and painted. They're all out there recapturing their youth, aren't they, and you can't blame them for that!"*

CHAPTER THREE

THAT WAS THEN ...

Freedom! Mark Davies at speed on his Malaguti Monte, Flackwell Heath, Buckinghamshire, summer 1977.

BOOM!

The 1970s is now recognised as a golden age for motorcycling in the UK. The sixteener market, created by the Government in 1972, was a major factor in creating a two-wheeler boom in the middle of the decade. Total motorcycle and moped registrations in 1975 topped 270,000, up from less than 128,000 in 1971, and there were more than 272,000 sales in 1976, and over 265,500 in 1977. Sports mopeds were essentially a stop-gap for novice motorcyclists itching to move on to bigger and better things, or a way for teenagers to get mobile 12 months before being able to take to four wheels. In reality, they represented a great deal more than that to many thousands of young people.

For half a generation aged 16 between 1972 and 1979, or 1980, it was as influential a part of their lives as being a mod or a rocker in the 1960s. A whole generation of motorcyclists started out on sports mopeds. A huge number of today's bikers fall into that band, and the sports moped generation currently forms the backbone of the British biking community. A great number of present-day motorcyclists are in their forties, and comparatively few younger men and women ride superbikes. In the 1970s, there were many superbike riders in their twenties.

Riding a sports moped was a superb introduction to motorcycling, and was the first rung on the ladder to a Kawasaki Z900, a Suzuki GT750, or even a Moto Guzzi Le Mans, or Laverda Jota. Thousands more moved from their mopeds straight to cars, but they still look back on their moped year with nostalgia and affection.

Generally speaking, sports mopeds were competent little motorcycles. They were, on the whole, good looking, balanced, and sweet handling machines. Riding them was great fun. In addition, they gave sixteeners symbolic and tangible freedom after years of bicycles, lifts, and public transport. It was a time of transition to the adult world. For most, their moped year coincided with leaving school and beginning to make their way in life. Riding a motorcycle felt grown up, it offered instant credibility, and it was a great way of impressing people, especially girls.

The country's school bike sheds and college car parks were full of little motorbikes with pedals, and there was something that bonded their owners together as a group, something beyond the fact that they all had age in common, something it was great to be a part of. There was a camaraderie and a spirit of adventure. They were 16, and they were 'the lads' (mostly). Their world was beginning to open up.

A unique combination of factors brought about the sports moped phenomenon, and the motorcycle sales boom it helped fuel. Ironically, the catalyst was the Peyton legislation, drafted in 1971, which, it could be argued, was designed to make motorcycling unattractive to beginners.

"Everybody thought the 'sixteener law' was a bad thing, but that didn't turn out to be the case. The fact that beginners were restricted to smaller more manageable motorcycles, because that's what sports mopeds were, became a good selling point. Eventually, it created more sales because once lads got a small bike they got the bug, and kept going." - Peter Padgett.

"The 'moped law' was a good thing for the industry. It opened up a new market, and created an affordable way into motorcycling. When the law came in all that were available were NSU Quicklys, etc. They were what old and sensible people rode, and that's what the Government had in mind for us. Then the sports mopeds came out, bikes like the Yamaha FS1-E, which was similar to the YB100 already available. It was a big improvement on what was already there. The first

Kids and 'peds. (Courtesy Rob James, Keith Bell, Steve Quiney, Charlie Owens, Ian Gregory, Gerry Croxson, Andrew Molyneux, Barry Moore, Jon Ridley, and John Barnes)

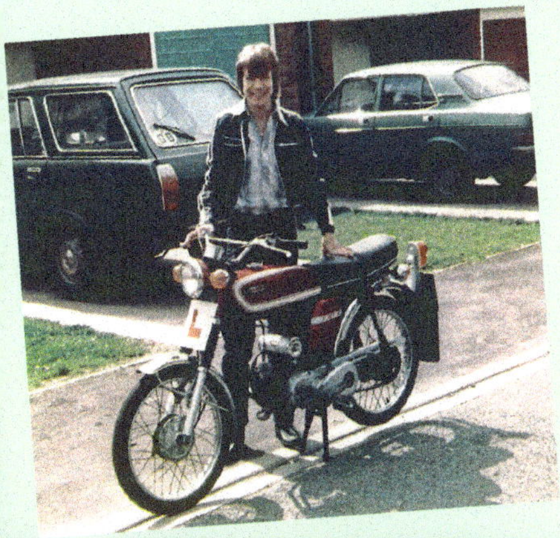

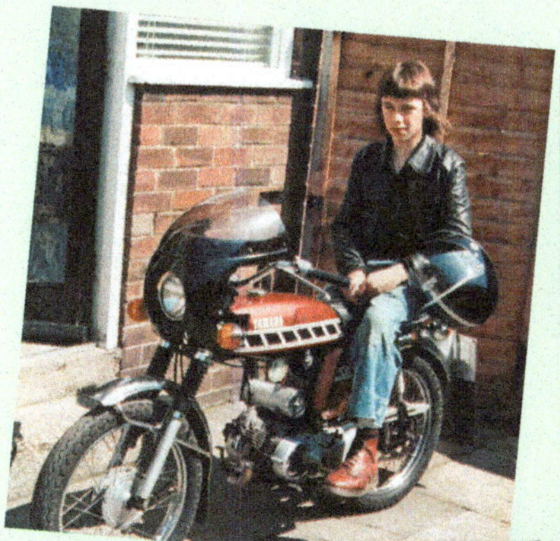

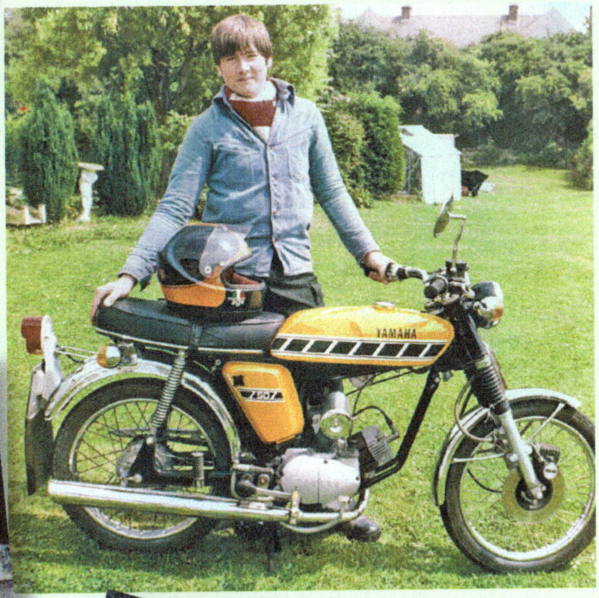
YAMAHA

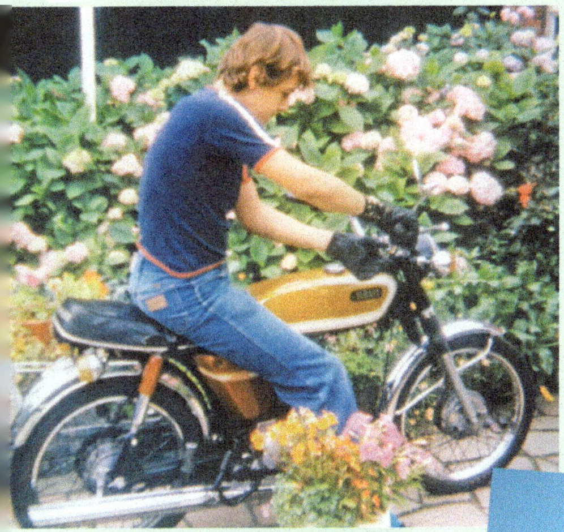

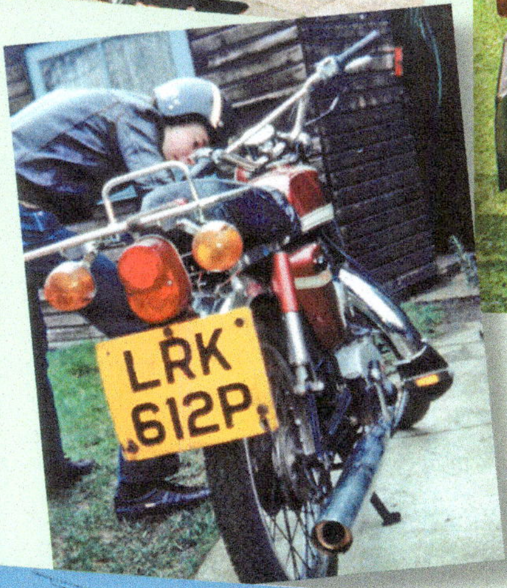
LRK
612P

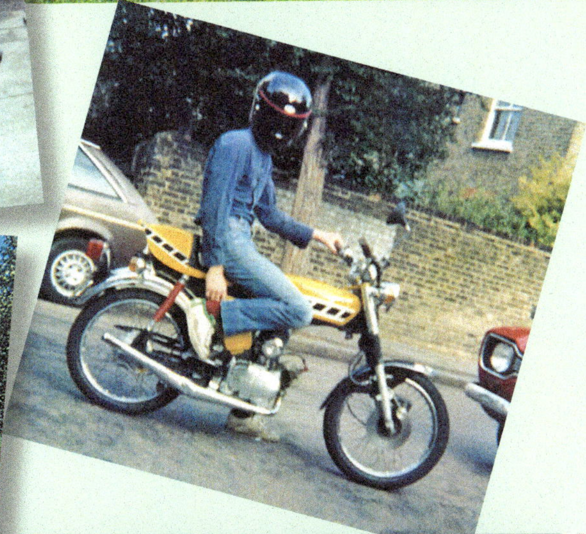

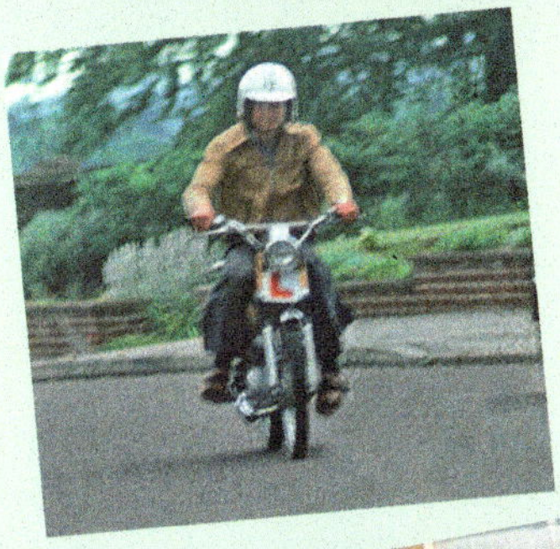

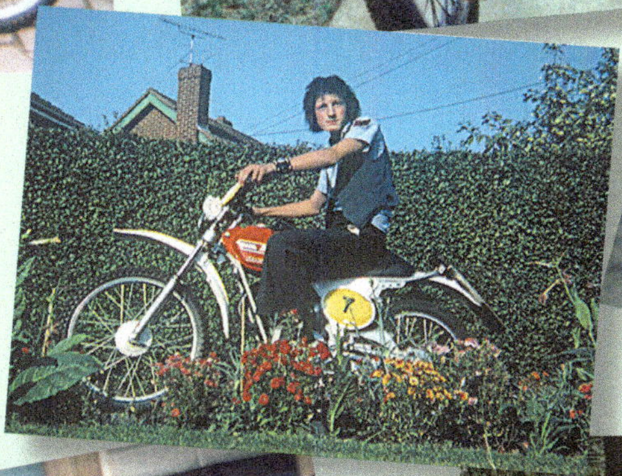

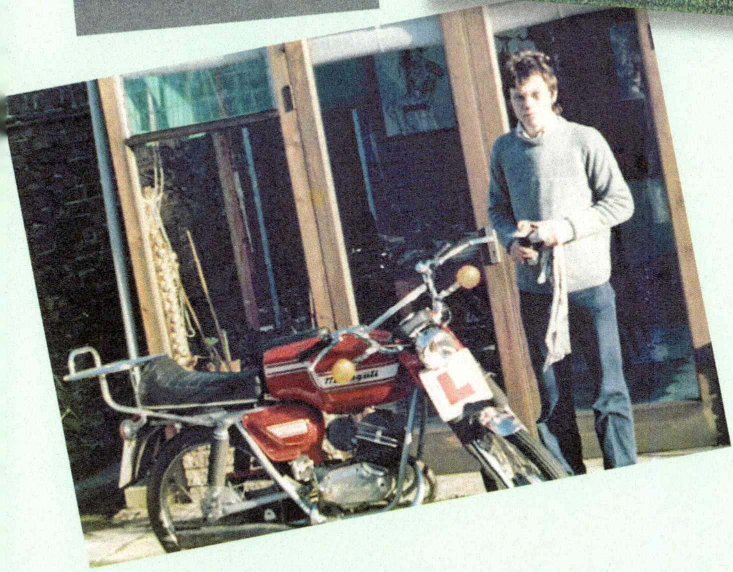

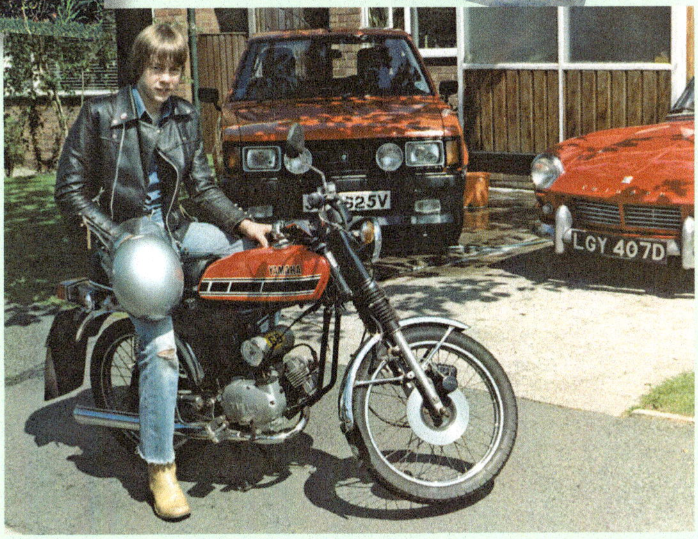
LGY 407D

Funky Mopeds

gold SS model came out, and sales were phenomenal. I sold 40 of them in 1973." - Terry Silvester.

"Before the legislation, you could have a 250cc bike at 16, and there was no moped market. Those who weren't into bikes would wait until they were 17 and get a car, but when the sixteener law came in it inadvertently hooked people into biking. They got a sports moped to be like their mates. There was an *esprit de corps* among mopedists, and they wanted to be part of the scene." - Brent Fielder.

There was also peer pressure of a kind that had never existed before. From 1 September 1972, teenagers began staying on at school a year longer, and, at the same time, 16-year-olds began turning up at school on mopeds. This was extremely impressive to kids approaching 16, and helped drive sports moped sales. Apart from the attractiveness of freedom and belonging, there were also down to earth economic reasons why seventies sports mopeds sold in such great numbers.

"Motorcycling's a leisure activity now, but in the seventies people used them as a practical way to get to work. 16-year olds were leaving school, and there were jobs for them to go to. They needed transport, and mopeds were a good way for them to get to work. It was also fun, a culture thing. Kids hung around together, and rode together, in their spare time. Owning a moped became an attractive thing to get into." - Terry Silvester.

GETTING IT TOGETHER

It's debatable whether 'sixteener specials' were more affordable than restricted scooters and mopeds are today, but hundreds of thousands of 16-year-olds in the 1970s found the money somewhere to get a sports moped on the road. Some were lucky enough to have rich parents, who bought them a bike. Others saved up enough from part-time jobs to buy a second-hand machine on their own, or scraped together a £30 deposit and persuaded a parent to sign the HP papers as guarantor. In the 1970s, it was possible to buy a second-hand moped, tax and insure it, and be on the road for £200. This was including a year's insurance at less than £20, and the annual road tax of £2.50. Terry Silvester remembers selling dozens of insurance 'pad policies' across the counter at £18 a time, making £2 or £3 on each. Typical HP payments were £2 or £3 a week.

Paul Simcox began saving up for his Garelli Tiger Cross long before his 16th birthday. "I got mine three months early from Perry's of West Bromwich. My mum had said 'over my dead body,' but I worked for my dad, and saved up. I was fortunate - all my mates bought theirs second-hand or on HP."

Charlie Owens, from Derbyshire, also got his moped before his 16th birthday. "I bought mine in 1977, when I was 14. It was a wreck. I paid £30 for it and did it up. I remember the speedo was missing. I saved up for ages and ages until I had £20 for a new one. I still get bits from the bloke I bought it from. I sold it to a mate in 1980, but by that time it was a wreck again."

Chris Mahon worked as a cleaner, and had a factory job to save up for his Fantic Super T. He bought it from his older brother when his brother had finished his moped year, and moved on up to a Suzuki Hustler six months before Chris's 16th birthday. "I got a short-term bridging loan from my parents, but I was saving up like mad, and I'd paid for the bike long before my 16th birthday."

Confirming Terry Silvester's point about bikes for work, Steve Fitzsimmons, from Ferrybridge, needed transport to get to work. "I started work as a miner when I was 16, and I needed a bike to get to the pit. My parents bought it for me, and I remember it was delivered to the house, and it started raining so I put it in the kitchen."

Gerry Croxson's parents also bought their son a sports moped for travelling to and from work, but knew bikes are for fun, too. "My dad had quite a few bikes when he was younger, including a Vincent Black Shadow, and he had a motorcycle and sidecar when he and my mum got married. When I got a moped he was really tickled, and rode it round and round the garden with my mum on the back."

Chris Alty, secretary of the Sports Moped Owners' Club, had his first bike bought for him by his father, despite his father's reservations about him riding bikes on the road. "My dad was a motorcyclist when he was younger, and he did his best to stop me getting involved because he got knocked off by a drunk, and left in the gutter. It was no good as I was already into motorcycles, and had decided what I wanted to do."

Russell Sears, founder of the FS1-E website, used his candy orange FS1-E to get to college after leaving school. "Like a lot of people, I had a lot of trouble persuading my parents it was a good idea, but I managed to convince them and scraped up £110. Then I scoured the papers and found the SS."

Russell Marsden helped his mate, Malcolm, negotiate to buy his M reg FS1-E for £25 and a diver's watch! "It had been crashed a couple of times so it was cheap. Mally had a go, and we struck the deal, and then we set about looking for second-hand switchgear and the other bits it needed. We rebuilt it and sprayed it in his kitchen when his mum was out, and that's how I got to know his sister Margaret." Russell and Margaret Marsden are now the owners of Fizzy Galore, the one stop FS1-E shop.

WHICH MOPED?

From its small beginnings in 1972, the sports moped sector

That was then ...

The Garelli Tiger Special. A facelift model available from January 1976.

grew to become the largest in motorcycling, and by July 1976, there were 46 different sixteener models available from 17 manufacturers at prices ranging from £189 to £329. What made some models more attractive and popular than others? Looks, reliability, and performance were obviously important, but availability was also a factor. With their dealer networks already well established, Japanese manufacturers sold their products across the whole country. The Yamaha FS1-E was the national best seller, but Garellis and Fantics were also popular wherever there were outlets, and Malagutis, Puchs, and other makes sold well in some areas.

Garelli

"In Goole, there was a local Garelli dealer, and because of that there were plenty of Garellis. When you're 15 or 16 you can't travel far to look in bike shop windows." - Brent Fielder.

Steve Fitzsimmons, a miner from the same area, bought a red and black Garelli Tiger Special. "I wanted a Garelli. Everybody had 'fizzies,' but I wanted to be different, and I knew they were faster. I hung around at Senior's Motorcycles on my Raleigh Chopper until I got one of my own. FS1-Es were sensible people's bikes. I don't like sensible things."

Paul Simcox was 16 in January 1976 "The Tiger Cross really caught my eye. Two people had them near where I lived. When I realised they were mopeds I thought I'd just got to have one."

"It was 1973, I was 15 and I took part in the Herefordshire County football trials. Among all the pushbikes in the car park was a Mk I Garelli Tiger Cross. I thought 'Christ, what's that?

It's got pedals.' I fell in love with it there and then. It just hit me, and I had to have one. The feeling I had about that bike has never left me." - Neil Holland.

Brent Fielder was also smitten by the Garelli Tiger Cross, but had to wait until he was nearly 17 to own one. "I was 16 in 1973, and I was already on the road on a Mobylette. One day I saw this little yellow moped with knobblies. It was so fast I just couldn't believe it. I nagged and nagged my parents for one, but as I got near to my next birthday I stopped. Then, two or three weeks before I was 17 my dad told me he'd ordered me one. My nagging had backfired in my face."

Neil Holland was 16 in December 1973, but he had to wait until the following April before getting his Tiger on HP. "I persuaded my uncle to sign as guarantor, but I saved up the deposit and paid for it myself. I used it for 18 months, and sold it, which I regretted straight away."

Julian Kowalewski went into his local Garelli dealer as a schoolboy, and saw a Tiger Cross displayed on a shelf on the wall. "It looked stunning, and I knew I wanted one." Julian then got a job pruning poplars for £20 a week, throughout the summer of 1977, so he could buy his Garelli Tiger Cross when he was 16.

Honda

Chris Alty now races 50cc two-strokes, but he started his motorcycling career on a Honda SS50 four-stroke. "I got a second-hand Kermit green SS50 5 speed from ACME Motorcycles, in Skelmersdale, when I was 16. It wouldn't have been my choice, but my father was buying it, and it was a sensible bike. People used to say 'An SS50? Oh deary me, never mind.' It wasn't the fastest sports moped around, but my dad and I did some work on it to make it quicker."

"The Garellis were always among the fastest, but even

Garelli's Rekord Mk I and Tiger Cross. The Rekord's 19 inch rear wheel gave it a top end edge, but the Tiger Cross had better acceleration.

Funky Mopeds

The 5 speed Honda SS50 was faster than the earlier 4 speed model, but still went chuff-chuff-chuff!

Dealers couldn't get enough Yamaha FS1-Es.

then we knew the Hondas and Yamahas were more reliable, and better built. However, the Garellis were physically bigger, and more like a proper motorcycle. The Honda SS50 4 speeds had grey frames and short bars, and were desperately slow. The 5 speed version was a lot better, but it still went chuff-chuff-chuff." - Brent Fielder.

"The SS50 was slow, always at the back of the pack, but there were a few around. Some people bought it to be different, others because their dads wanted them to have a 4-stroke." - Russell Marsden.

Yamaha

"There was nothing wrong with the SS50, but it didn't appeal to the boys as much. It was a precision motorcycle in its day, but Yamaha bettered it. We used to sell all the Japanese Sports mopeds and the Garelli Tiger Cross, but most people wanted the Yamaha FS1-E. They sold like hot cakes, it was amazing. It was a success from the start. It was instant. People just walked into the showroom and wanted to buy them. We didn't have to sell them." - Peter Padgett.

"The FS1-E was the king of the street in the 70s, and still is now. More people had FS1-Es than any other sports moped, and that's still the case. They were popular in the 70s because Yamaha was a known make, and they had the engineering edge over Italian stuff and Casals, etc. FS1-Es had a proper ignition system, indicators, and mirrors, and were the best value at the time. The Suzuki AP50 wasn't around until later. The Honda SS50 was out early, but had no time to build a reputation before it was swamped by the popularity of the FS1-E." - Russell Marsden.

"The FS1-E was the definitive sports moped, the bike everybody wanted to have. It seemed to me, when I was 16, that it was the 'fizzy' everybody was trying to copy. The Garellis were faster, but the FS1-E was more reliable, and to me the Suzuki AP50 looked dated as soon as it came out." - Russell Sears.

Fantic

Chris Mahon has never forgotten the first time he saw his brother's Fantic Super T, the bike he later bought for himself. "When he brought it home, and parked it on the lawn. My jaw just dropped. I couldn't believe it – it was a lovely little thing. A proper little motorcycle. It had huge fins, and carb, and a b****y great exhaust. 'You can't ride that', I said 'It's a 125'. My brother said 'Look, there are pedals on it, Chris!'. Then he started it, and it went 'bang-ber-dang-dang-dang!' The noise was incredible, and that attracted me to it even more because my nature, at the time, was to be antisocial and cause annoyance whenever I could. I was a bit of an a******e really! I loved that noise, I really loved it. I loved the bike, really."

"Garellis and Fantics were definitely more antisocial, the Fantic Chopper incredibly so. The original wasp trapped in a coke can." - Brent Fielder.

Barry Moore had an AP50, but has always been a Fantic fan. "It's the noise they make. They always seem to sound great, and they're very quick."

Gilera

"Gileras were good little bikes, but a bit slow because they had tiny inlet and transfer ports. Unrestricted bikes without

That was then ...

Fantic Caballero. Big bike looks and one of the fastest mopeds around.

pedals had the same engines, but were a lot quicker. Basically they took a responsible line, when they interpreted the UK sports moped regulations." - Chris Mahon.

"I got a Gilera by default. I hadn't even considered motorcycling, but when I left school my mum and dad took me to Goddards, an old fashioned bike dealer in High Wycombe. My dad said 'Right, now you're an apprentice you'll need transport, and we're buying it for you.' Unfortunately, the bike they'd chosen was a Puch Maxi, complete with shopping basket! I was mortified. I said 'No way, I'm not riding that b****y thing.' Anyway, Goddards sold Gileras, so I talked my mum round to getting me one of those, and she persuaded my dad. They got me a red Gilera Touring." - Gerry Croxson.

Steve Wilkinson, from Dunstable, saved up for his Gilera Touring by working in a petrol station. "The styling was attractive to me, and I'm still a fan of Italian bikes. They're not necessarily clever motorcycles, but they're built with passion rather than with a business head. The Fantic TI was very popular and very quick, and so was the Garelli Tiger, though it was clearly a budget bike. I chose the Gilera."

"I would probably have never got a bike, a car was always the plan, but I was well aware of the moped scene. My mates were starting to get bikes, and kids a year older than us had hung around outside the school on Garellis and Fantics, when we were in our last year. So, when my parents offered to buy me a bike to go to work on for a year, I persuaded them to get me a Gilera. I enjoyed it so much I kept it for two more years, and had two more motorcycles after that." - Gerry Croxson

Gileras. Good looking and well built, but a bit slow.

Puch

John Dunn, from Nottinghamshire, spent most of his sixteener year on FS1-Es after starting off on a Puch M50 Sport, and it was another Puch, the black and gold Grand Prix Special, that caught his attention above all other sports mopeds. "A lad called Kenny Hawkins had one in a neighbouring village. It looked really different in those colours with cast wheels. You rarely saw them, and they were quite a lot of money when new. I just had to have one, and many years later I did."

Casal

Fizzy Galore boss, Russell Marsden, bought a Casal ST50 eight months before he was 16, but tried to trade it in for an FS1-E two months after getting it on the road. "I was bored with it, and decided to buy an L reg gold SS for £120 from Earnshaws Motorcycles, in Huddersfield. They didn't want

Fantic Super T; small and antisocial!

Funky Mopeds

Rich boy's toy, the Puch Grand Prix Supreme.

the Casal, in part exchange, because they thought that poor parts availability would make it difficult to sell, so I took the SS, and sold the Casal in the *Huddersfield Examiner*."

Gitane

Cumbrian Mark Wilson had two workaday FS1-Es and an exotic Gitane Champion Veloce. He used the FS1-Es for night riding and long journeys, and the Gitane for scratching.

"Even though I had a great time on my SS50, it would not have been my choice. I wanted a Gitane Champion, despite the fact a friend at the time had one. It was frighteningly unreliable, the bulbs blew constantly, and the brakes squeaked all the time." - Chris Alty.

TAKING TO THE ROAD

Now you're living with Casal. The Portuguese company's 1975 advertising campaign.

For most sixteeners, becoming mobile was instantaneous and a wonderful thing. Unlike today no training was necessary, and it was possible to ride unaccompanied from the very start. For many their first day on the road remains one of the best days of their lives, a fantastic feeling burned into the memory. It even got better: commuting to school or work, and riding for fun with mates in the evenings and at weekends. Getting from A to B had never been so much fun!

"They were happy days, fantastic times. I remember my 16th birthday. I said to myself 'Yes! My life starts now!'" - Paul Simcox.

"I got my bike a few days before I was 16, but I didn't sneak out on it before the day. On my birthday I was up at 5am. It was a gorgeous sunny August morning. It was an incredible feeling. The whole day stays in my mind." - Chris Alty.

"I remember thinking 'It's great this!' It was brilliant. We were out on them all the time. We got home from school, or work, and couldn't get our tea down fast enough. It was a case of in, change, tea, helmet back on, and off." - Russell Marsden.

"We'd moved on from pushbikes, got these little bikes, and become adults. We had wheels, and suddenly we could go places and do things we couldn't do without them." - Russell Sears.

"It was a fantastic thing because instead of relying on a pushbike, or the bus, or something like a Mobylette, we had real independence, and we were free on the road for the first time. I could go to York, which was 20 miles, and sit on the river bank, and chat girls up, or ride to the coast. A gang of us even did a 150 mile round trip to Cadwell Park." - Brent Fielder.

"When I collected my bike from the bike shop, the owner, Mr Goddard, insisted I learned some basic skills by riding round a car park before he'd let me take the bike away. When he thought I was good enough, I crawled home really slowly, but it was a fantastic feeling, amazing. It was elation I suppose. For ages I used to think 'My God, I got here in two minutes, it used to take me half an hour!" - Gerry Croxson.

"Riding a bike changes your life. The faster you ride the more it comes together and flows. It changes your persona." - Chris Mahon.

"They were crazy days, and we rode every day in all weathers, happy just to be out. We rode everywhere. I used to ride the bike to school, get thrown out, and spend the day riding." - Steve Wilkinson.

"It was a really good time. I felt independent, and for the first time in my life I didn't have to rely on buses, or lifts from my parents." - Neil Holland.

"There's nothing like motorcycling. The boys got a moped, and had fun on them straightaway. They rode around

That was then ...

Perhaps the most exotic of all sports mopeds, the Gitane Champion Veloce.

together in groups, and they were bikes for work, as well. It made going to work fun, too." - Peter Padgett.

PACK CULTURE

Seventies sports mopedists rode in packs, often as many as a dozen in a group, and they were out at every opportunity, every weekend, and almost every night. They rode hundreds of miles a week, but usually never ventured more than a few miles from home, and often went out just for the sake of riding. Chip shops, youth clubs, car parks, and village greens were regular destinations. Anywhere to stop, and have a chat and a fag, before racing back again. Motorcycle showrooms were popular places to call, even though sixteeners were often treated disdainfully by dealers and more senior customers.

Sixteeners rode for miles in all weathers, through wind and rain, and in the freezing cold of winter. Even with faces too frozen to talk, and fingers and toes too numb to feel the controls, burning up the streets and lanes was fun, and addictive. Riding sports mopeds was about freedom, friendship, exhilaration, competition, and speed.

"There was a real moped scene. Everybody had one. Every town had a crew hurtling about. There were all types of bikes. We used to congregate at the Wimpy drive-in, in Dunstable, which was basically a hut." - Steve Wilkinson.

"We hunted in packs. Everybody went to the chip shop or down the Wimpy. There was a lot of camaraderie, but also a lot of competition - everybody thought they had the fastest bike. There was a piece of road in Watford we called the strip. It was a section of dual carriageway. That was the proving ground. You could see them lining up - it was like that scene in Grease." - Russell Sears.

"Everyone and his brother had one. My close friends had a Tiger, a Rekord, a gold FS1-E, a Malaguti Olympique, a Cavalcone Cross, a Fantic Chopper (he had a rich dad), and an SS50 4 speed. We rode around together in a big pack, as many of us as we could get together. The Tiger was always one of the fastest, but the Rekord had a slight top end edge, maybe one or two mph. We hung around the chip shop, and the youth club, and we took them to school, and to work." - Brent Fielder.

"There were so many mopeds about, it was unbelievable. The place was inundated with FS1-Es and Garellis. Every 16-year-old seemed to have one, and there were gangs everywhere. Everybody wanted to race you, didn't they?" - Neil Holland.

"There would be up to 20 of us on mopeds, meeting up in Skelmersdale, at a place we called 'the bench'. Lads came from all over the town and beyond. Nobody phoned anybody up. People just appeared, and we went for a ride, though we never got very far. Just around the town really. It was just that

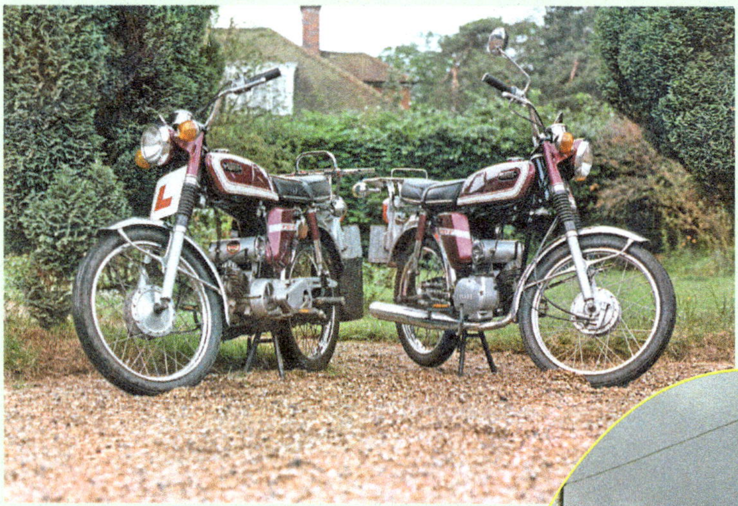

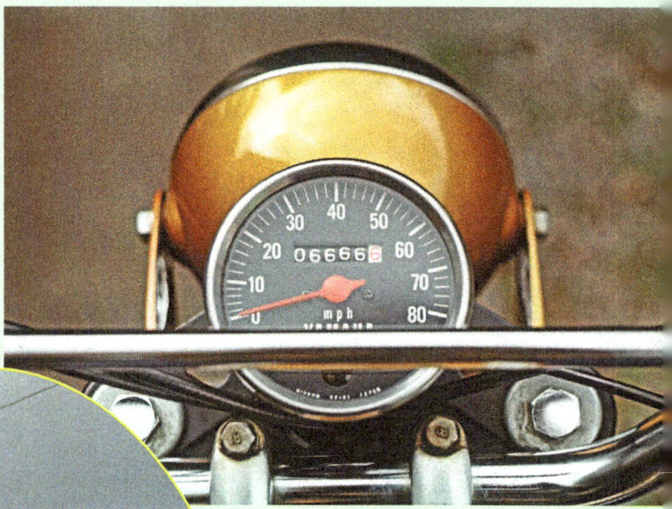
30 40 50
20 60
10 70
0 80
06666
mph

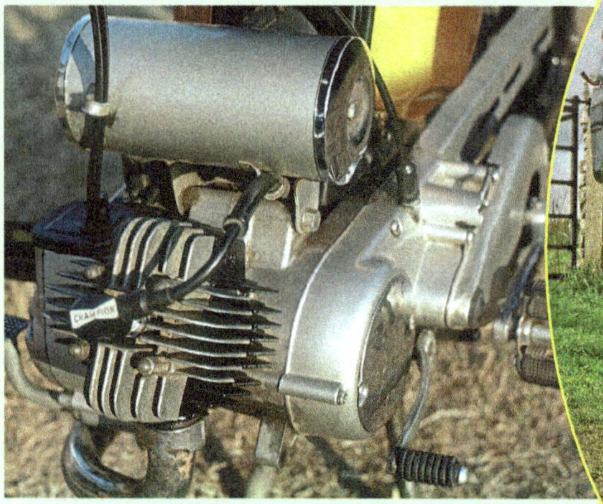
CHAMPION

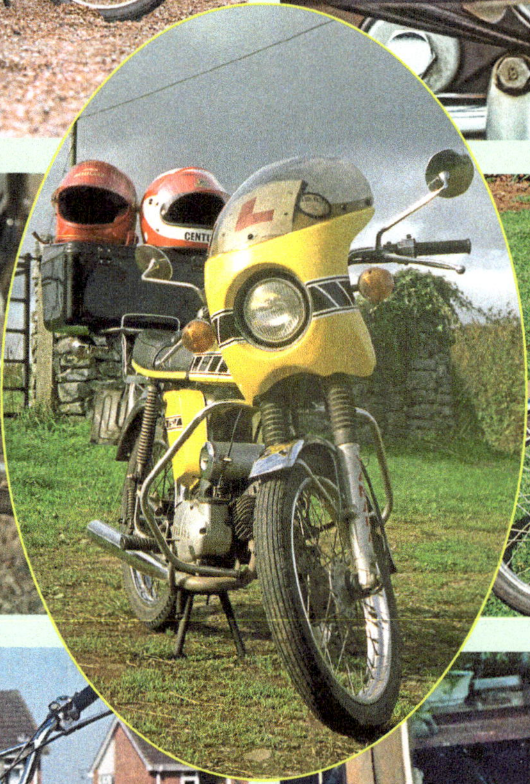

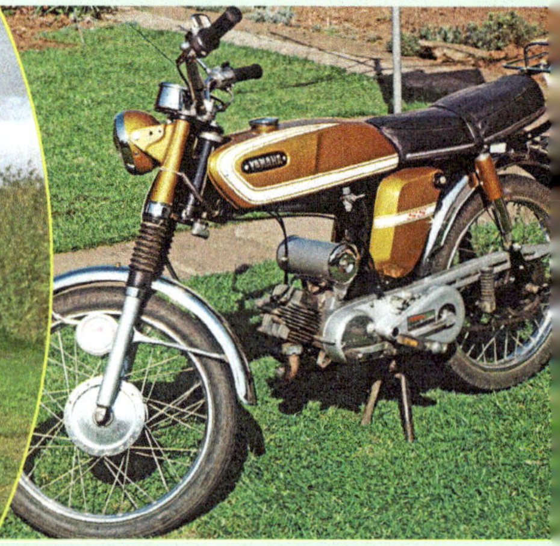

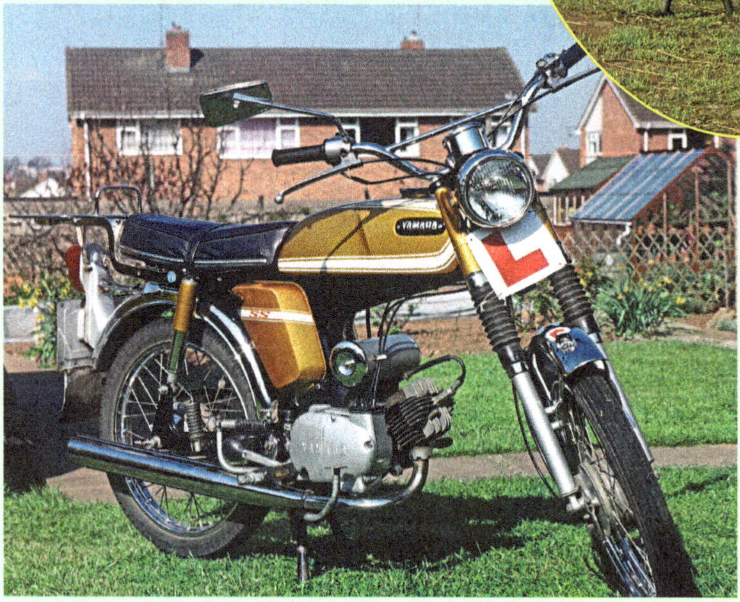
YAMAHA

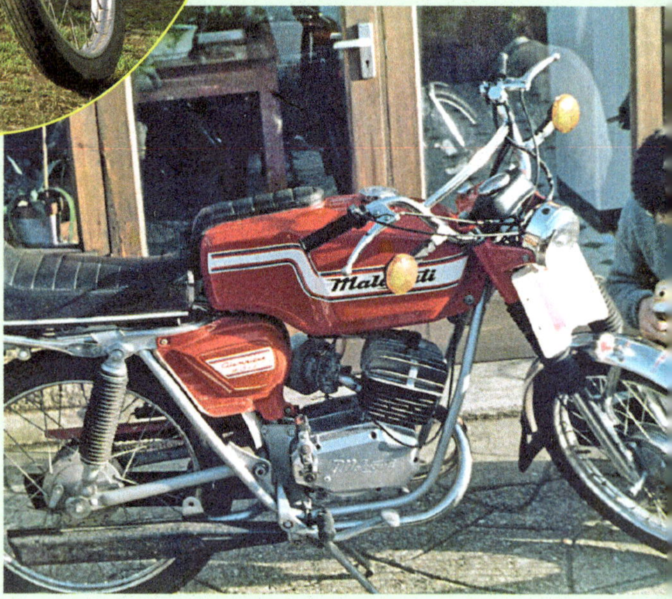

That was then ...

there was an attraction in being together." - Chris Alty.

"Did we race? Ooh yes, but there was nothing to touch my Tiger Cross. I had six mopeding friends. Two had FS1-Es, and four had Italian bikes, Gileras, and Garelli Rekords, but nothing could keep up with my Tiger. FS1-Es had good initial acceleration, but I overhauled them. The Honda SS50 four-speeds were pathetically slow." - Paul Simcox.

"There was incredible rivalry. Everybody claimed to have the fastest bike. There was a stretch of dual carriageway where we used to challenge each other. It was slightly uphill, so we raced both ways." Chris's Honda SS50 5 speed was tuned, and could take on all comers. A lad called Ian Newton, who went on to be a successful road racer, was certain his Suzuki AP50 was quicker than Chris's bike. "'Newt' needled me for a race, and in the end I accepted. I slaughtered him mercilessly, but he got back to 'the bench' first, and told everybody he'd won." - Chris Alty.

"There would be as many as 15 of us, but there was no Italian stuff in our gang. We'd go down the chip shop. The Suzuki AP50s were quicker than the FS1-Es. My mate, who was 16 before me, had an FS1-E DX, and I chased him on my Raleigh Grifter. Then, when I was 16, I blew him off on my AP50." - Barry Moore.

"We were always in tens, or whatever, and I had mates on AP50s, FS1-Es, Fantics, Malagutis, a Yamaha TY50P, and a Flandria, which was a rarity. They were sold at Woolworths, but we had a dealer around here, Lockside Motorcycles, of Castleford. We met at 7pm, and rode around the cafes and bike shops. We didn't go to pubs. We hung around the square and at phone boxes. The furthest we went was Selby Fork Services on the M1, or Sherburn Coffee Bar, which has been a bikers' cafe since the 1950s." - Steve Fitzsimmons.

"We'd arrange what we were doing the night before, and usually it was a case of calling for friends, hanging out for a while, then going off in a group of seven, or eight, for a burn up to the next town, or village, or to a chip shop, or the youth club." - Russell Marsden.

"We went down the chippy, and hung out behind the supermarket, and all that. Though some of us were a bit more adventurous. Every Sunday night a group of us would ride down to the cinema in town, known as the flea pit, and watch films like Easy Rider, Death Race 2000, and Smokey and the Bandit. The films went round and round." - Gerry Croxson.

SIXTEEN AND STUPID!

Putting Redex petrol additive in the tank to create a massive plume of smoke from the exhaust, or injecting lighter fluid

Period 'peds. (Courtesy Andrew Bishop, Ian Gregory, Jonathan Ridley, Robert Gardiner, John Barnes, Paul Treneary)

Night rider. (Courtesy John Barnes)

Burning it up to the chip shop. Rivalries were intense. (Courtesy Keith Bell)

straight into the carburettor to get a phenomenal surge of power are two of the more ridiculous things 16-year-olds did to their mopeds.

On the whole though, the stupidity was confined to racing around like idiots. Although the buzzing about no doubt irritated some people, it was still a time when getting into trouble meant a clip round the ear from your dad, and as a result there wasn't much truly antisocial behaviour.

Like all 16-year-olds they thought they were immortal, and rode as though they were. Inevitably there were casualties, but accidents were usually at fairly low speeds, or the result of losing control of a wheelie, or other stunts gone wrong. They were generally fairly minor, but racing was an everyday occurrence, and sometimes there were tears before bedtime.

Julian Kowalewski on his Tiger Cross and his foster brother, Rob, on his Malaguti Cavalcone went out in the Herefordshire lanes looking for cars to blow off, but only managed one successful overtake. Julian remembered "We found a Reliant Robin, but it took an eternity to pass it!"

"I remember one of us (name withheld), drunk, pulling a massive wheelie along the length of the shop fronts in the village on his Honda SS50 5 speed, with his feet dragging on the ground. The police saw him, and tried to stop him, so he rode off, turning his lights off to get away. The same bloke was on the back of his SS50, two-up on a country lane, with another mate of ours riding the thing. The road had been resurfaced, and they got themselves onto gravel swept up into the middle of the road. A car came the other way, and Mr X baled out, off the back. The guy on the front lost control and went down. The bike smashed into the car and was totally wrecked. Neither the rider nor the car driver was insured so Mr X returned to the scene later with a hammer, and bashed up a tree to fabricate an insurance story, and to satisfy his old man.

Funky Mopeds

TRIAL GILERA

TOURING GILERA

That was then ...

A few months later the same bloke seized his Suzuki GT185 solid after running the oil tank dry." - Gerry Croxson.

Gileras, like a lot of Italian mopeds, didn't have an ignition switch. Gerry Croxson again "I came out of the youth club one night, and someone had started it up and left it ticking over. Nearly all the petrol was gone; it must have been running for over an hour. The same night someone broke into a mate's purple Cortina GT Mk II and hid it round the corner."

"The Garelli had no ignition, but I used to ride it to Tech one day a week and leave it in the car park all day. It was never nicked." - Steve Fitzsimmons.

"The exhaust on my Tiger got blocked up, so I cut the pipe off to let it breathe. What a racket! She flew for a bit until I blew it up!" - Julian Kowalewski.

"I used to ride through a subway, with the kill button held in, and let the engine fill up with fuel. Then I'd let go of the switch, and Bang! Hey, we were 16 and stupid!" - Steve Fitzsimmons.

"My older brother asked to borrow my SS to go to the off licence. I said 'OK but be quick, I'm just off for a ride'. An hour later, he reappeared pushing it back. The bars were bent, a lever was broken, and the headlight was trailing on the floor. He said 'Sorry, I got into a tankslapper', a tankslapper? It wasn't an H2 Kawasaki. No way did he get into a tankslapper. He was drunk, and he'd crashed it. It wasn't his first visit to the off licence that day. He disappeared for four days after that, too frightened to face my mum and dad." - Chris Alty.

"There were crashes, but nothing too major for most of us. Just bouncing across the kerb, that sort of thing, carrying on from scrapes on pushbikes." - Brent Fielder.

"I vividly remember the first day on my FS1-E. My uncle picked it up in his van and brought it home for me. The next day I took it out and rode it up the road, but my mind was so preoccupied with the clutch and gears, etc., I couldn't work out how to get it round the first corner. I went straight on across the kerb, and into a set of railings. Thankfully the only thing that was damaged was my pride." - Russell Sears.

"I got into trouble with the police for aiding and abetting a friend's drunk driving, looning about on the back of his Tiger Cross." - Neil Holland.

"When I bought my FS1-E, I was happy with it, but it had a nasty back tyre so I deliberately made it bald as quickly as I possibly could, and changed it for an Avon." - Russell Marsden.

Paul Simcox and his mates went to Worcester on a camping holiday, a 70 mile round trip from Birmingham. "A group of 18 of us went to the seaside, but only ten made it there and back. There were allsorts. About ten FS1-Es, three AP50s, two Honda SS50s, a Garelli Tiger Cross, a Fantic, and a Casal."

"A group of us went to watch road racing at Cadwell Park. It was a 150 mile round trip, and it took us so long to get there we arrived just as the racing finished. We had breakdowns, and people ran out of petrol. We borrowed washing lines to use as towropes, to keep going." - Brent Fielder.

POLICE

Despite being young and occasionally very stupid, most seventies sixteeners got along with the police, though sometimes people found moped gangs a little intimidating, and the police were asked to break up groups at their meeting places.

"We had problems with the police, but it was just sheer numbers that gave cause for concern. We used to meet near the centre of old Skelmersdale, and although there was an occasional guy wheelying his FS1-E, on the whole we behaved ourselves. The Chief Constable and the Residents' Association decided the only suitable place for us was a wet weather pitch, out of town. It was a bit bleak, and there was nothing to keep us there, so it wasn't successful." - Chris Alty.

"We had a village copper, PC Miles, and he was forever moving us on from behind Budgens (small local supermarket). One day Andy, one of the group, gave my mate Gary a lift the mile or so from his house, to Budgens on the back of his FS1-E. Andy hadn't passed his test and Gary didn't have a helmet. He just put his coat hood up. Gary hopped off outside Budgens looking rather pleased with himself, but moments later PC Miles pulled up behind them in his panda car. He radioed the station, and they called Gary's mother, who came up and gave him a right ticking off. PC Miles didn't book them, or anything, just let them off. That's the way the police did things in those days. Gary was shaking with fear and embarrassment when he knew his mother was coming. He never lived it down." - Gerry Croxson.

"We had a good relationship with the police. They treated us like adults, and we appreciated it. That's what it was all about, thanks to these bikes, we'd become adults." - Russell Sears.

SPEED

So how fast were these little machines? There are a number of factors clouding the issue. Firstly, to put it tactfully, there was a great deal of exaggeration and wishful thinking at the time, about what speeds had been achieved. Secondly, all moped speedometers gave optimistic readings. Most of the Italian clocks were ludicrously inaccurate with needles that fluctuated insanely. Thirdly, most 16-year-olds were ultra-lightweight specimens able to wring a few more miles per

Left: Gilera's early advertising promised freedom and excitement.

Funky Mopeds

hour out of a moped, than could be achieved with an adult on board. Finally, a lot of 'quick' mopeds were tuned, and had altered gearing, or even oversized engines.

Of the more popular mopeds, the Fantics and Garellis were the fastest in standard trim, managing a genuine 60mph on a level road, and up to 10mph more downhill. A Yamaha FS1-E would do an indicated 48mph on the flat, which was, in reality, 45mph. Downhill, chin on the tank, left hand on the fork stanchion, feet on the rear footpegs, changing up the box by hand, it would reach 55mph tops. Suzuki AP50s were a little faster, but no match for the Italian stallions.

"On sports mopeds the power to weight ratio is critical, and 16-year-olds are generally light, often around nine stone, but even so, 60mph is good for a Fantic. Nothing on a Garelli speedo counts at all!" - Chris Mahon.

"The speedo on my Tiger was all over the place, but it'd do a genuine 60 on the flat." - Brent Fielder.

"Garelli speedos are wildly optimistic. My Rekord does 57/58mph, but shows 70 on the speedo! The Rekord is about one mile per hour faster than the Tiger Cross because of different gearing and wheel sizes." - Paul Simcox.

"The Rekord had a 19in rear wheel which gave it the edge on top end, and the Tiger had better acceleration with its 17in wheel." - Brent Fielder.

"Realistically an FS1-E would do 45mph on the flat. That's all. You have to remember the speedos were optimistic." - Charlie Owens.

An untouched FS1-E would do 50/55mph downhill, flat on the tank, and 48mph on the flat. Any slower and it needed a decoke." - Russell Marsden.

Mark Wilson claims he could wring nearly 70mph out of his six speed Minarelli P6-engined Gitane Champion Veloce, one of only two sold in Carlisle. He said *"It was very high geared, and took a lot of winding up. It didn't like hills, no moped did, but it was a fraction of the weight of an FS1-E, and it could fly."*

"The tuned fizzies were fastest down the strip, in Watford. It was the very early days of sports mopeds, so there weren't expansion chambers and tuning kits, as such. The work on them usually consisted of porting improvements, skimmed head, and a Hepolite piston. The baffles were either discarded or cut in half." - Russell Sears.

Nothing on a Garelli speedo counts at all!

TUNING

In every town in the UK in the 1970s there were young home mechanics, who spent hours in their parents' garages fettling and filing, and swapping standard parts on their mopeds for go-faster goodies, sent in the post from tuning companies advertising in *Bike* or *Motorcycle Mechanics*.

Results varied, and many home tuning efforts were disasters, but John Dunn, from the North Midlands, made local newspaper headlines when he was stopped for speeding at 68mph, between Tibshelf and Morton, on his doctored Yamaha FS1-E DX. *"They're the smallest-engined vehicles you can buy, and it was a challenge to make it go faster."* remembered John. *"It was certainly fast when I finished. A little flying machine."*

John bought his specialist parts from Beeline Racing, and his modifications included ace bars, bump seat, expansion chamber, different gearing, reworked and oversized barrel, larger piston, skimmed cylinder head, altered timing, modified disc valve, larger carburettor, and resin in the crankcases "to squeeze the mixture". Surplus parts, such as indicators, were removed to save weight.

Parked up out of sight in a number of favourite spots around his Nottinghamshire village, John would wait for the sound of other mopeds approaching, then pounce and blow them into the gutter on his demoralisingly fast fizzy.

A totally illegal, but effective and easier way for John to achieve such substantially increased performance would have been to swap his engine for a Yamaha YB100 motor (not unknown). Or he could have opted to tune his FS1-E DX a little less extremely by restricting himself to filing out the ports, rejetting the carburettor, and cutting down the standard exhaust baffle. The usual result of carrying out these milder modifications was to produce a machine that would pull 60mph in top gear, but at the cost of losing some bottom end power.

Honda SS50s were easily upgraded by fitting 70cc, or 90cc, top ends from the then ubiquitous C50/70/90 range of step-through commuter bikes. Chris Alty rejected this option, preferring instead to tune his SS, but owners of bigger bikes sometimes beaten by the flying 50cc four-stroke, just could not accept it hadn't had a capacity hike. *"I once had a race with a guy on a Suzuki TS100 trail bike."* remembered Chris. *"The SS was a match for it, and he just couldn't take it. He couldn't accept it didn't have a larger engine, but that would have been unthinkable to me. Increasing the performance, without increasing the capacity, was the challenge."*

Chris's father bought him the SS50 as a sensible choice for a first bike, but didn't mind helping his son get more performance from the bike. *"My dad and I gas flowed the*

That was then ...

Companies advertised tuning parts and accessories for FS1-Es, in the motorcycle press.

cylinder head, fitted a larger carb off a CB125, I think, and we made a new inlet manifold for it. It went like the clappers! We didn't raise the gearing, and I shudder to think what it revved to, but it went to well over 60mph, was still phenomenally economical, and it never let me down."

Home tuners were in the minority, in the sports moped fraternity, and there was none in Brent Fielder's gang. "The bikes were entirely standard. Most of us just didn't have a clue."

PROS AND CONS

Sports mopeds were able machines, and light years ahead of most step-throughs in specification, but let's not get carried away. It was still difficult to keep up with fast traffic, their riders were buffeted by trucks, and overtaking was definitely a risky business. Also, sixteener specials were built to a budget, and we're talking about 30-year-old technology, here. The electrical systems on most of the continental machines were inferior to the Japanese models, and six-volt electrics meant headlights like hot nails. Speedometers were ludicrously optimistic, and two-stroke oils of the time meant regular decoking was essential. Japanese tyres were hard wearing, but not especially grippy (did the ribbed fronts on FS1-Es ever wear out?). Trials and motocross knobblies offered poor grip, especially in the wet, and disc brakes didn't work in the rain, in those days. Braking performance, in general, wasn't up to car standards, even in the dry.

Nonetheless, there were some true classics, like the great all rounder, the Yamaha FS1-E, and the more basic and feisty Garelli Tiger Cross, There were exotic machines, such as the Gitane Champion Veloce, conservative bikes like the Honda SS50, and some oddballs, none odder than the Fantic Chopper. What were they like to live with?

"The FS1-E's build quality was very good, there was a good spread of power, and the electrics were better. On the Gilera, if you used the horn at night the lights went out because the magneto wasn't up to the job." - Steve Wilkinson, Gilera rider.

"The Garellis, and other Italian bikes had no battery, no neutral light, and no stoplight, or provision for one - and they were more expensive. The FS1-E was a better bike." - Charlie Owens.

Garelli Tiger Cross owner Neil Holland rode his mate's FS1-E, and remembers it being smooth and comfortable, compared with his Garelli, with the gears well spaced. "I thought b****y hell it's a much better ride, but I preferred the Tiger, the FS1-E style wasn't to my taste. I preferred the trials-type machines."

"The Garelli was a much simpler bike than the Japanese stuff, and the electrical system was inferior, but the engine was in a relatively high state of tune, and it made plenty of power." - Brent Fielder

The Tiger Cross had plenty of power, but not a lot of torque. "You had to work it all the time to keep it at its peak. One duff gearchange, and you'd lost the lot." - Paul Simcox.

"Fantics vibrated a great deal because we were revving the crap out of them, all the time. My Super T shrieked like a little racing bike, and I just revved it and revved it. They were pretty uncomfortable to ride, but it was bearable because of the short distances we did." - Chris Mahon.

"Fantic Choppers are fast, and the handling's surprisingly good. The brakes are okay, but you have to use the back brake more than normal. The front is spongy because it's got a long cable, but the back brake is very effective." - Barry Moore

Fantic Caballero magazine advertisement, March 1976.

No pedals on these European model Tiger Cross and Rekord machines.

Funky Mopeds

Fantic's exotic Chopper.

MAINTENANCE & RELIABILITY

Ridden flat out all the time, most sports mopeds were remarkably reliable considering the abuse they received, but some were more reliable than others. Although there are some protesting voices about this, it seems fair to say that, on the whole, the Italian bikes were not as dependable as the Japanese machines, unless they were meticulously maintained, which is not something 16-year-olds are known for. Checking the gearbox oil and frequent decoking was about the only mechanical attention most mopeds received.

There were exceptions, however, particularly among those now involved in the sports moped revival scene. Unlike most moped riders, who had no real mechanical aptitude, or knowledge at 16, Paul Simcox undertook two full engine rebuilds on his Garelli on his own. In fact, having got the bike three months before his 16th birthday, he completely stripped it and pulled the engine apart *"Just to see how it worked."*

Pedantic about his Fantic, Chris Mahon would drop the oil every two weeks, passing it on to a grateful mate, who would use it in his own moped.

Russell Marsden carried out his first FS1-E restoration in 1978, while he was still 16. He swapped all the painted parts on his gold SS to change it into a purple FS1-E, and rode it like that for six months, while he saved up to buy new parts from Padgett's of Batley. Once he'd assembled everything he needed, he pressure washed the bike, stripped it, and rebuilt it, respraying his gold paintwork. *"It was an early Jurassic restoration, but I did it with genuine bits, and I used Padgett's own aerosol paint. I masked off the pinstripes, gave it layers for depth, and then lacquered the lot including the stripes. I took a full week's holiday, and when I went back, my employers said they must be paying me too well – they thought I'd bought a brand new bike!"*

He continued *"My dad had had a scrapyard, and I was always messing about with spanners, taking things apart, to find out how they worked. I had rebuilt and repainted a few pushbikes when I was 14 or 15, so I was fairly confident, but not as far as splitting the crankcases."*

"I was always taking the head off the Gilera, and decoking it, but not once did it break down nor need any parts replacing. The only problem I had was a loss of power in the first couple of months, but the dealer solved that by sawing the innermost end off the exhaust baffle. It went fine,

Echoes of Lotus's John Player Special Grand Prix cars, in Puch's black and gold top of the range model, the Puch Grand Prix Supreme.

again, after that." - Gerry Croxson.

Yamaha FS1-Es were renowned for their toughness which made them a popular bike in the motorcycle trade, as well as with customers, but other manufacturers' products enjoyed a less enviable reputation.

"A lot of FS1-Es were neglected, people just couldn't be arsed. Fortunately, they were extremely tough little bikes and put up with a lot of abuse. It's really hard to blow a gearbox

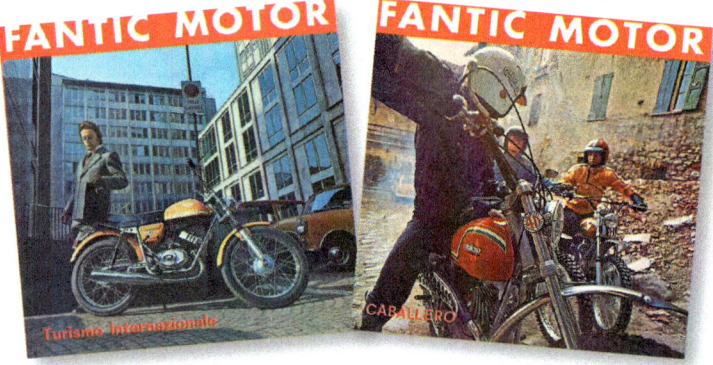

Early *Fantic Motor* sales literature.

That was then ...

on an FS1-E, they were extremely robust." - Russell Marsden.

"The Yamaha FS1-E was first class in every way, both in appearance and manufacturing quality. It was a hardy and reliable bike, but we sold a lot of spares because people crashed them, and the oils weren't as good as they are now." - Peter Padgett.

"They were easy to fix at the side of the road. I always carried a spare plug and basic tools in case a plug whiskered up, or the points gap needed adjusting, or the carb got flooded." - Russell Marsden.

"Fantics could be fast, but they were temperamental. If the timing wasn't exactly right, it would affect the performance drastically. Were they reliable? No b****y way. They'd make you cry, when you found yourself pushing them home again and again. Sometimes there'd be inexplicable breakdowns - they just wouldn't go. No reason could be found, then they'd be alright again"

"Piston rings would break up at quite low mileages, and bits would just b****y fall off. Nuts and bolts would come undone - the exhaust heat shield bolts would just fall out, exhaust nuts on the barrel would come loose, the toolbox cover lid would just drop off, and bounce down the road. If you were fortunate, and heard it over the racket of the engine, you could go back and get it. A lot of the problems were just down to vibration really." - Chris Mahon.

Paul Simcox champions the Garelli marque "My Garelli was reliable, until I altered the timing to make it go faster. It was successful, but I knocked the bottom end out twice after that."

"When we were 16, we didn't do any maintenance, and Garellis responded to that by filling their exhausts with carbon, and getting slower and slower. It would also have paid to have kept an eye on the timing. The points and plugs needed attention, or they would become unreliable. The points would close up and the plug would whisker. The main problem was they were thrashed to within an inch of their lives. Garellis have got a chrome plated bore so they couldn't be rebored, if you dropped a ring, or the chrome started flaking off. A new barrel was needed." - Brent Fielder.

"There was a guy around here who had a red Garelli Rekord, and he was always pushing it up and down the road - but that's what owning a Garelli's all about, isn't it? They were temperamental. You'd go to a dance, ride it there and it wouldn't miss a beat, come out and it wouldn't start. All the FS1-E riders would have their bikes running, and they'd be saying 'Come on Neil, b****y hurry up!' The FS1-Es were reliable. They always started." - Neil Holland.

"Yamaha FS1-Es were reliable, but they didn't go fast enough. Garellis fell to bits. The back mudguards snapped, I had two under warranty, and the flywheel fell off when the woodruff key sheared. The woodruff key was made out of monkey metal, you'd be better off making one out of a penny! The bike went back to Agrati, the Garelli importers in Nottingham, when that happened, and it was rebuilt with a new crank, piston, and barrel - but the turnaround was good, it was only off the road for a week.

"Garellis were built to a price, but like Fantics, they went like s**t. Gileras never broke, but they didn't go either, and SS50s were probably the most reliable of all, but they were absolutely dog slow." - Steve Fitzsimmons.

Decoking two-stroke mopeds, and burning the baffles off, became a regular ritual for sixteeners intent on maintaining or improving performance. The job consisted of scraping the carbon off the piston crown and the inside of the cylinder head, and polishing with Solvol Autosol, cleaning carbon deposits from the exhaust ports, and pouring petrol over the exhaust baffle and setting fire to it. The really keen would leave caustic soda in their exhaust pipes overnight to eat away at the grunge inside.

"We were forever decoking them, but there's no need today as two-stroke oils are so much better." - Paul Simcox.

"Now they don't need decoking because fully synthetic oil burns so clean, and they're reliable because we do ongoing maintenance. Nowadays, with better plugs and fully synthetic oil there are fewer problems." - Brent Fielder.

The Honda SS50 was the only four-stroke sports moped, and like Hondas, in general, it had a reputation for reliability. Chris Alty's SS50 was modified for extra performance, but still ran all year without problems.

"The only thing that happened was the screw inside the gear selector drum came loose, once, causing sloppy gearchanges and misselection. I just had to take the clutch cover off to fix it. It was easily done." - Chris Alty.

PEDALS

Pedals on sports mopeds were a token gesture and a bit of an embarrassment. At best they were impractical, and some didn't work at all. That was not the point, however. Apart from MoT testers, and the occasional vindictive copper, nobody really cared if the pedals worked or not. The pedal systems were purely a device to get round the law.

"The pedals were used as footrests. It was a good idea, but it was all a con. They were all difficult to pedal. Some were impossible." - Terry Silvester.

"On the Garelli Tiger, you put it into fourth and pedal frantically to keep in motion. After 20 yards you're out of puff, and fall over in a heap. You could say it's a struggle." - Paul Simcox.

Fantics were possibly the most difficult of all to pedal.

Funky Mopeds

There were a number of different pedalling systems, but they all had one thing in common - they were purely a device to get around the law.

That was then ...

"To pedal a Fantic Super T you had to swing one pedal round and lock it in the opposite position to the other, but there was nothing to disengage the pedalling mechanism from the engine. You had overcome its compression, and keep the kill button pressed while you struggled along." - Chris Alty.

"It is just about possible to pedal a Fantic Chopper. You put it into sixth, pull the clutch in and pedal like mad. It's not easy though nothing fouls. The Gilera was the easiest to pedal. The FS1-Es and AP50s used to slip and snatch." - Barry Moore.

"Pedalling a Gilera was awful because the exhaust pipe was in the way. A wobbly two mph was all that could be achieved." - disagrees Steve Wilkinson.

"Lanky kids would have to pedal fizzies bandy legged, because their knees kept hitting the bars. We'd pedal them sometimes for a laugh, and they had to be working because a vindictive copper might demand to see you pedal it, and do you, if you couldn't." - Russell Marsden.

COOL DUDES

Apart from tearing around on their mopeds, seventies sixteeners were also busy discovering girls. Brut 33 was splashed all over, and Denim was the mark of a man. Like teenagers of all generations, it was vitally important to look cool. School ties were worn with enormous knots, and the trousers had huge side pockets. Jeans had four inch turn-ups, and shirt collars could take someone's eye out. There were shoes like table tennis bats, and platform soles that made gear changing impossible.

"We wore what was fashionable, certainly not motorcycle gear. Oxford bags, big collared shirts, and stupid shoes." - Russell Sears.

"We had flares so big we could walk in them without disturbing the material." - Gerry Croxson.

"Trousers with 47 pockets and a million buttons, a tank top with a star on it, a Boeri helmet, and an Ashman leather jacket with tassles." - Steve Fitzsimmons.

"We wore Falmers jeans with huge turn-ups, and leather bomber jackets with elasticated waists and cuffs. I had driving gloves with black and white check across the knuckles, and an open back. Checked lumberjack jackets with white fur was another favourite." - Brent Fielder.

"Jeans, and bomber jackets, and Salacio shoes." - Paul Simcox.

"Trench coats were de rigeur, and Stadium helmets with stickers all over them. I remember that Stadium Project 6 helmets were £5.95, and there were Centurion open face ones, which had a leather bit at the back. They were always covered in stickers and bits of tape." - Steve Wilkinson.

"I had a 'Keep The Faith' Northern Soul Club Roadshow

Cool dudes.

clenched fist sticker on the toolbox of my Garelli." - Brent Fielder.

TRAINING AND TESTS

Very few sixteeners took their moped test. It just wasn't worthwhile, as the only advantage was being able to carry a passenger, and the test had to be redone after graduating to a proper motorcycle. As a result, most youngsters didn't even pick up a copy of the highway code until attempting to pass their motorcycle, or car test, a year or so later.

Gerry Croxson was one of the few who made the effort to take the moped test. "I did it because I didn't like the loony plates, I hated them. I went to Slough to do it because the test route was on the flat there, and easier than the nearer hilly

A natural progression: 1973 Yamaha FS1-E to 1975 Yamaha RD200 Electric. (Courtesy Russell Sears)

45

Funky Mopeds

one in High Wycombe. I passed, but the only problem then was I was always getting collared to give people lifts."

Chris Alty represented the majority. "I really couldn't see the point. Two-up meant going slower, and the test didn't mean anything once you turned 17."

Most sixteeners wobbled off into the traffic for the first time without any training, but some dealers were responsible enough to offer a degree of basic tuition, before letting newcomers loose on the roads. Paul Simcox's headteacher insisted that the moped boys in his school did the Star Rider training course, and some parents had the same idea. There was also an RAC/ACU Motorcycle Training Scheme, originally introduced in 1947, which comprised six evening theory sessions and six Sunday mornings spent riding round cones, in a council car park, and being shepherded by instructors in small groups on the road. There were written and practical tests at the end of it, to earn a certificate and badge.

WHAT HAPPENED WHEN WE WERE 17?

Riding a motorcycle with pedals was embarrassing enough at 16, but it became completely unbearable at 17, and for most the love affair with the sports moped was over as soon as that birthday was reached. It was time to move on. Some said goodbye to two wheels and learned to drive a car, but bitten by the motorcycling bug, a great number bought their first real motorcycle.

At the time, mopeds could be converted to motorcycles by removing the pedal mechanism. In this form, they would have been easy machines for 17-year-olds to pass their motorcycle tests on, but very few utilised the option. Ludicrously, reclassifying the machine as a 50cc motorbike as much as trebled the insurance, and after a year on a moped, everybody was itching to move on to bigger and better things.

"When we were 16, there was a group of 17-year-olds, with RD250s, who didn't want to associate with us. We were from a much lower class, and we could only talk to them when we'd got rid of our mopeds. So when we turned 17, we couldn't wait to get on a 250." - Chris Alty.

"When we were 17 there was a split, half to cars and half to bikes." - Brent Fielder.

"It had always been the plan to have a car, and I'd had one on the driveway for six months before I was 17, and passed my car test as soon as I could. I actually kept the Gilera for quite a while afterwards, and I ended up buying two more bikes when I was a bit older." - Gerald Croxson.

"When we were 17 we didn't want anything to do with mopeds. I refused to reinsure mine, I thought it was crap all of a sudden. I wanted to move on, the love affair was over." - Chris Mahon.

"When we were 17, we couldn't wait to get rid of them and get a proper bike. A real bike with a proper kickstart!" - Steve Wilkinson.

"We dreamed of an RD250, or GT250, then a Z900." - Brent Fielder.

"When I was still 16, I bought a Honda CJ125 with a screen and top box, a super sensible dodderer's bike. My 17th birthday was on a Saturday, I passed my test on the Honda on the following Monday, and by Thursday I had a Kawasaki KH400 triple. I've always done things differently." - Steve Fitzsimmons.

For those continuing with motorcycling it was a case of selling, or part exchanging, the 'ped, and for most, taking out HP on a real motorcycle. Inflation was high, in the mid-seventies, but it helped hold up second-hand values well. New bikes could be up to 20 per cent more expensive, but the loss in value when selling, or part exchanging, a machine was minimised as a result.

"You never lost much in a year because inflation took care of some of the depreciation. Bikes that were well looked after didn't lose a lot." - Peter Padgett.

The bikes most seventies 17-year-olds chose were the Yamaha RD125, 200, and 250, and Suzuki GT125, 185, and 250 two-stroke twins, and the Kawasaki KH250 two-stroke triple. Honda's CB200 and CB250 250 four-strokes were staid and dull by comparison, and there was no real non-Japanese alternative. Whatever bike was chosen, it was time to learn, and learn quickly, that riding with the throttle wide open at all times was no longer a good idea.

For those who switched to four wheels, it was time to master the art of hillstarts and reversing around corners in their Escorts, Cortinas, and Avengers.

One way or another, the boys of the sports moped generation put their sixteener year behind them (for the moment), and began to make their way in the world ...

www.veloce.co.uk
Details of all Veloce books • New book news • Special offers • Newsletter

CHAPTER FOUR
... AND THIS IS NOW

"Wa-hey!" Charlie Owens gives a Garelli Tiger Cross a blast across a Derbyshire field.

Paul Simcox and his thirty-year-old Fantic Chopper. (Courtesy Paul Simcox)

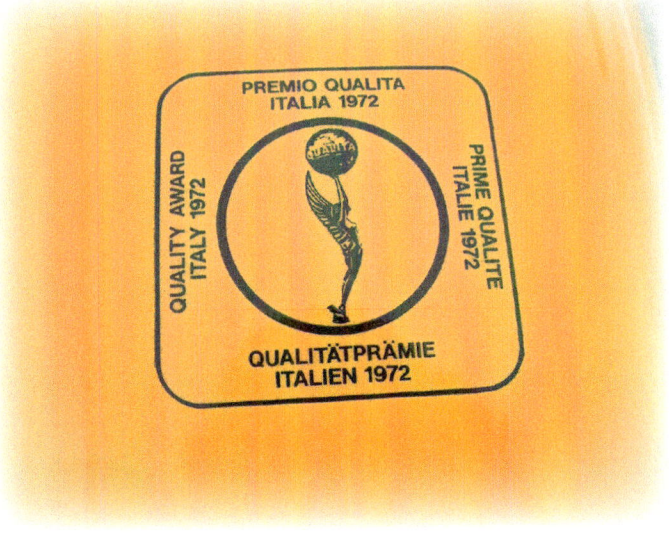

Still mopeding after all these years! (Courtesy Paul Walton)

PURE NOSTALGIA

Sports mopeds are steeped in meaning, and incredible nostalgia is aroused by them. They are little time machines with the power to evoke happy memories for the thousands of now middle aged men who rode them in the 1970s. These little bikes can carry them back to their youth, to a happy and carefree time.

Seventies sports mopeds on the road today attract attention. Bikers toot and wave, and give the thumbs up, and riders are flagged down for a chat. One restorer was stopped by policemen because they wanted to talk to him about his bike! Bikes on display at shows and exhibitions draw wistful looks, spark nostalgic responses, and attract offers of hard cash.

"The first time we rode a bike is right up there with the first time we made love. Most of us with sports mopeds are back on our first bikes. That's what's in it for me. I've got the bike I had when I was a teenager, and I ride it on sunny days."

Brent Fielder: *"When I ride along and look down at the tank I feel 16 again."*

Funky Mopeds

It takes me back. When I ride along and look down at the tank, I feel 16 again. My advice to anyone with a sports moped is do some serious miles, and enjoy it." - Brent Fielder.

"It all stems from the fact we had good times on them, and it takes us straight back to the mid-70s when we all left school, and had freedom for the first time. Ninety-five per cent of people with a 'fizzy' today had one when they were 16. Most people keep one and run it in good weather, for old times' sake." - Russell Marsden.

"Everybody wants what they had when they were a kid, don't they? That's why Raleigh Choppers are collected and valuable. We've all got to 40, we've got kids, and houses, and cars, and perhaps a bit of spare money, now, so we can indulge ourselves." - Charlie Owens.

"The bikes weren't missiles, but they gave us our first taste of freedom, and we can taste it again, quite easily. We can relive it, and, through the Sports Moped Owners' Club, team up with people who did it at the same time. It's pure nostalgia, and it's affordable. You don't have to spend a lot of money." - Chris Alty.

"Our generation has certain things in common. We can all remember when 'Cum on Feel The Noize' went straight in at number one, we all got beaten up by the PE teacher, and we all remember the year on our mopeds. Our first independent transport. A great time. Having one again opens the door to the past, it's nostalgia." - Chris Mahon.

"My teenage times were not particularly good, and my Garelli Tiger got me out of the house and away. It symbolises freedom for me even now." - Julian Kowalewski.

"Motorcyclists who didn't start in the 70s couldn't begin to comprehend it. They mean nothing to people who didn't experience them. At the first Stafford show SMOC attended, we put an interesting stand together with a Fantic Chopper, and Garellis, etc, and some guys in their fifties came up, and started sniggering. One said 'Why on earth are you bothering?' On the next stand were 15 identical BSA Gold Stars and nothing else. We had an incredible variety. Another problem is bikers in Britain are a bit sizeist, whereas on the continent 50cc bikes are popular and more commonplace." - Chris Alty.

"Many people suffer from big bore bike problems. They're overbiked! People think that if their bike's not 1000cc, it's not a proper bike, but very often these big sports bikes are too much. These little ones are fun to ride again, and people are really enjoying riding them." - Steve Wilkinson.

"I've had a lot of big bikes, but in recent years I've had more fun with mopeds. Bikes are too fast now, and I can't resist using the power. If you hit something at 120mph plus you're dead, aren't you? I've had friends killed on bikes recently." - Steve Fitzsimmons.

"I enjoy riding a moped in itself, but also the nostalgia

The author's Gold SS FS1-E. Many restored mopeds have a pampered existence.

of it. Riding mopeds is definitely not about a need for speed. If I've had a bad day, I don't go for a thrash on the fizzy. I go out on my Fireblade. I ride a big bike every weekend, and also my two-stroke 250s and 350s. I get a very different thrill out of riding them!" - John Powell.

"When I park up on a mint moped, people come up to talk to me. They invariably say 'I used to have one of those', or 'I always wanted one of those', or 'my mate used to have one of those', or 'I don't believe it. I haven't seen one of those for years!'" - Brent Fielder.

"People love to reminisce. I had a Garelli Tiger Cross on the back of a pick up, and I was driving down the A1 when a Mercedes passed me, jumped on the brakes, and waved me down. I thought there was a new speed camera, or something, but he just said 'I hope you don't mind, but I want to look at the bike. I had one of those when I was 16.'" - Steve Fitzsimmons.

"I've got over 1000 customers, and they're all different sorts of people, but they've all got something in common. They

... and this is now

had an FS1-E when they were 16, and now they've got one again, and they're reliving their youth." - Russell Marsden.

"When a group of us went to Sherburn Cafe, all the guys on big bikes came over and started bowing. They were all our age. We were all lucky to have been sixteen in that narrow window." - Brent Fielder.

"Being on the Sports Moped Owners' Club stand at the Stafford bike shows takes me straight back to my teenage years, and people keep coming up to us and saying 'It's like going back in time, here'. If we take some mopeds to Sherburn Milk Bar everybody flocks round them." - Steve Fitzsimmons.

"It was a short-lived time. We're an elite club. We just happened to be the right age, at the right time." - Russell Sears.

"The seventies was a good time. People still want to talk to me about the bikes I sold them. Some people I do remember, and some I don't. Only a couple of weeks ago someone came in to buy a bike and said 'Do you remember selling me my FS1-E?'" - Peter Padgett.

Gilera expert Steve Wilkinson adds a dissenting voice. "I have to confess to a certain amount of disillusionment. It seems so much smaller and slower. I thought I used to bomb about everywhere, but apparently not. But then again, I'm four stone heavier, and the traffic's a lot quicker nowadays."

RESTORING, COLLECTING, AND RIDING

The Sports Moped Owners' Club was founded in 1996, and has gone from strength to strength. Interest is growing every year, and an increasing number of people are dragging mopeds out of sheds, and from under hedges, and restoring them to their original or, in some cases, better than original state.

Like all collectors, sports moped restorers are on a mission to preserve something from the past, and the desire to recreate the time of their youth is a powerful and passionate emotional force. It's partly about an urge to discover things, and it's also about appreciating beautiful things. There aren't many motorcyclists who don't enjoy bikes as objects of art, and some sports mopeds are truly funky little motorcycles. What's more, owning them now transports those who also rode them in the 1970s straight back to an idealised version of their teenage years.

Collecting is also a neurosis. It's an inability to let go, a desire to deal with the complexity of the world by doing something to bring about order of some sort. In this case, something positive, but unconventional. Then there's the excitement of the hunt for the bikes and for spares, the joy of success, and the satisfaction of rebuilding and recreating something both attractive and meaningful, and the friendships forged with fellow enthusiasts.

"The restoration itself is pleasurable. It's getting that last

A good restoration candidate?

elusive part, finishing them, and getting them running again. Then I can sit back and say, 'I've done that, I've brought another one back to life.' Then there's the chasing bit – tracking down the bikes and the spares. If something's the right sort of money, I've often made up my mind before I've got there. It's also nice to see new faces, and to meet people with a common interest. I've got friends from all over the country, from Bournemouth to Scotland." - Barry Moore.

"I love putting them together. Once the frame's back, I do it bit by bit as I go along. A little bit of this and that, getting stuff chromed and plated, and bolting it on. I get a lot of enjoyment out of it, and it's as much of a hobby as riding the things." - Neil Holland.

"It's a challenge, and you've got to beat boredom somehow. You've got to have a hobby, it keeps you out of the pub." - Steve Fitzsimmons.

Restoring sports mopeds appeals to handful of people, a small percentage of a group, born in a small time window, men who were 16 between 1972 and 1977, and had these bikes, and have the time, skills, and confidence to rebuild one.

Some people recreate the bikes they had when they were 16, down to carrying out the same modifications, such as non standard bars, and adding the same accessories like racks and crash bars. Some produce a machine finished to a much higher standard than the original, but most go for the seventies showroom look. Some are ridden regularly, some only in perfect weather, some not at all.

Owned by a succession of super enthusiastic 16-year-olds, most sports mopeds were thrashed to death, and ended up on the scrapheap years ago, but the growth in interest in the genre in the 1990s has ensured that most of what has survived

Funky Mopeds

A Garelli Rekord Mk II before and after restoration by Paul Simcox.

will be saved. The relatively few surviving machines are now fetching strong prices when sold through the trade or between collectors, and pristine examples of some models are worth several thousand pounds. Fortunately, buying or restoring mopeds in a small way is still affordable for most people.

"The great thing about restoring bikes is you can do it in a shed or a single garage. To rebuild a car you need a double garage to do it properly." - Barry Moore.

"If you want to do up a Garelli, you can buy a wreck for a couple of hundred, and do it up at £10 a week over two years, and end up spending £2000 on it or, if you can afford it, you can buy one already done and ready to ride for £1500." - Steve Fitzsimmons.

Paul Simcox restores bikes to their original standard of finish, but enjoys riding them, and accepts they will become tarnished: *"95 per cent is good enough. The trouble with a concours bike is that if you get caught in the rain, you've got to take it apart again to clean it. I show them when they're first restored, then I prefer to use them."*

Barry Moore is also not sentimental about them: *"They go downhill if they're used, but they're not made to last forever, are they?"*

"I get great enjoyment from getting on a bike I've restored from the scrapheap, and riding it the way I need to ride it, ie flat out! I always get two of my bikes taxed and tested, and I use them through the summer. They're mint, but when I get back I spend a couple of hours cleaning, and drying, and lubricating them to keep them that way." - Brent Fielder.

Gilera expert Steve Wilkinson is knowledgeable about the small differences between the different models from the historic Italian marque, and the small changes made to the bikes, from time to time, throughout their production runs. He has striven for absolute accuracy in his machines. *"I enjoy discovering things, and finding out what's correct is very important to me. I like things to be authentic, if at all possible, and I try to improve them bit by bit, but I'm not a fan of concours bikes. I still like to ride the Gilera, even if it takes me an hour to clean it when I get back."*

"I take my fizzy out on sunny days, but I get more pleasure out of looking at it than riding it! I take it out sometimes, and put it on the drive, then I look at it from all the angles, then I clean and polish it, and put it away again." - Russell Sears.

*"I get a great deal of satisfaction out of riding them around. People pull up and say, 'B****y hell, I haven't seen one of them for years'. I can feel the enthusiasm coming from people. It's nice that people are interested and appreciate what I've achieved."* - Neil Holland.

"As soon as I park the Gilera, there's a crowd around it. 'Is that new?' or 'I used to have one of those,' are the most common responses." - Steve Wilkinson.

... and this is now

"I feel strongly I should use them for using them's sake. What's the worst that can happen? If the engine blows, it can be repaired. There's nothing made that can't be remade. They're not a work of art, they're mechanical devices that are designed to be ridden." - Brent Fielder.

Charlie Owens disagrees. His two mint condition early Yamaha FS1-Es are rarely ridden, usually only coming out for shows. He uses his modern Ducati superbikes for riding on the road. *"They look too good to ride. If I took one out and it rained I'd stop, phone my wife Sue, and get her to come and pick me up in the van."*

However, Charlie admits to being extreme. *"I'm an absolute perfectionist – I insist on the right washers, let alone the right bolts. I've spent hours studying the FS1-E parts book, and I'm afraid I'm fanatical beyond belief. I use nuts and washers from broken bikes from the same manufacturer and year, that way I know they came from the same parts bin as the missing ones on the bike I'm restoring. Even the seat bolts on FS1-Es, tucked away out of sight, have to be the correct 12mm items, not the more common 13mm ones used on many restorations."*

But Charlie is not satisfied. *"There are still some touches I would like to do. I'm always looking for improvement."* He would like to swap the correct, but new, rims on his purple FS1-E for rechromed original ones, but he finds himself reluctant to dive in and pull the wheels apart. Charlie puts this down to working with bikes full time, which understandably makes him less keen to work on his own machines in the evenings and at weekends.

Prolific restorer Barry Moore now allows himself to cut a few corners, but he started off using the parts book method on Yamahas and Suzukis, for absolute authenticity, sticking to the correct components, even if he felt he could improve the look of something by deviating from the original specification.*"I didn't have so much information on the Fantics and Garellis, so there was some guess work involved there, but with the Japanese bikes I knew what was right, and even if it looked a bit crap, I decided that's the way it was and left it. But no matter how hard you try, people will always stop you at shows and say, 'You've got the wrong bolt there mate.'"*

"I'm a true believer that if you're going to do it, you should do it properly with original Garelli bits. If I made do, and something wasn't accurate, It'd always bug me and play on my mind." - Neil Holland.

John Dunn's superb Puch Grand Prix Special has been rebuilt to better than new specification. John said *"I enjoy*

Regeneration. A new generation of sports moped riders following in their fathers' footsteps. (Courtesy Darren Bayles, Jonathan Ridley, Paul Walton)

Funky Mopeds

Restorer Ian Ritchie did a fabulous job on this Garelli Tiger Cross MkI.

paint colours can be matched accurately by specialist motorcycle paintshops, or even by restorers themselves if they're skilled and brave enough. Computer replicas of stripes, decals, and labels are often perfect and impossible to tell apart from the original items, whether home made by talented individuals, or manufactured by specialist firms such as Sunrise Graphics, a full time business devoted to reproduction transfers for Japanese bikes.

There is a certain cachet to having a bike with original paintwork: even with a few minor chips and dings, this feature can raise a bike's value over another example, even one with the most perfectly repainted tinware.

"There are some good paint jobs around, but you can't beat having the original paint on an early FS1-E. They just can't match it no matter how hard they try, it's the metalflake." - Charlie Owens.

trying to build the bike up to be as good as possible. It's about pushing myself to the limit, to try to achieve the best results possible."

"You can do too good a job. For instance, British chroming is better than the Italian or Japanese stuff in the seventies. I try to go for the factory look, to recreate the bike as if it was bought new in the shop." - Barry Moore.

"There are two ways to do it. As showroom condition or up a grade." - Neil Holland.

Sometimes practical improvements are sensible and don't affect the appearance of the machine. Mark Wilson's Gitane forks were seized, and when he stripped them he was appalled to discover the internals consisted of just a greased spring and a chrome rod. The Testi version of the bike he was using as a donor machine utilised car tailgate gas struts in its forks, so Mark put the Testi innards in his first restored bike, and is now looking for equivalent struts from car spares companies for his subsequent Gitane restorations.

Almost all restored bikes have to be repainted, and most

FINDING BIKES AND PARTS

All restorers and collectors dream of rare and sought after bikes turning up out of the blue, and in 1994 Chris Mahon found a 4 speed Fantic Caballero with just 42 miles on the clock. *"An old chap had bought it as a runaround. He hadn't passed his bike test and didn't want to ride with L-plates, but he could ride the Fantic on his car licence. Soon after getting it he became ill and died. His wife was unable to part with it for years, but she eventually sold it when she moved house. A local bike shop valued it for her, and put a steep price on it, but the provenance was so good, I didn't argue or hassle and bought the bike straightaway, unseen. We did the deal on the phone, and she said 'It's covered in dust, I'll clean it for you,' I said 'Don't touch it!' When I got there the petrol hose and grips had perished, but otherwise it was OK. A collector's dream really. The original warranty papers were in the tank*

... and this is now

John Dunn turned a rusty wreck into a showstopping restoration.

bag, not filled in, and it still had its original sparkplug, of course. She even gave me a seventies helmet, still in its box."

Mark Wilson, a Gitane fan, bought a Champion Veloce as a wreck for £200, after haggling for weeks, by e-mail, with a seller in Oxford. He got his own bike back after a chance meeting in a pub, and sourced a third from Scotland, which was rideable, but rough, with a lot of non-standard parts. Using parts from all three, he built an award winning show bike.

Barry Moore has mined the Nottinghamshire area successfully for years with adverts in the local free papers, and Neil Holland and Julian Kowalewski, from Herefordshire, scoured the county's bike shops, and advertised in local papers in the 1990s, turning up a blue Garelli Rekord in a barn for £25.

Neil thinks the supply is drying up fast, but Julian is more optimistic. *"I still think there are some unrestored mopeds about, here and there, because farming people don't throw anything away. There's an abundance of sheds, barns, and outbuildings, and some will have bikes in. They'll be rough, but they'll be there. I know where there's a Malaguti Olympique, in a shed, in the middle of nowhere, right now."*

Many early restorers found their bikes by advertising in local newspapers, and gathered spares at autojumbles and from bike breakers. Paul Simcox, however, has found most of his bikes and parts through detective work, and word of mouth, and has never advertised. Scouring old magazines, he has researched new area codes and prefixes to add to telephone numbers in advertisements, and contacted long retired dealers. Some still had spares at home, or in lock ups, and others provided leads that led to important finds. With his great knowledge and stock of spares, he has become an important figure in the sports moped restoration scene.

"The first parts I bought from Paul were some brand new Rekord headlights. After that, I've been forever ringing him up. He can get parts for all Garellis. He's the hub; he's the main boy really." - Neil Holland.

Barry Moore, who advertised for unrestored bikes throughout the 1990s, bought and sold moped parts to help pay for restoring them. *"I'd buy job lots at shops and autojumbles. I'd take everything they'd got, take out what I wanted, and sell the rest, so a lot of my bikes didn't owe me very much."*

It is becoming more difficult to achieve, but with care and a little shrewdness, restoring sports mopeds can still be a self-funding hobby. John Powell admits to using his knowledge of classic Yamahas to wheel and deal in spares, to fund his passion for FS1-Es, and the aircooled twins of the marque.

Now there are fewer bargains, as bikes and spares have become more scarce, and the trade has woken up to the renewed interest in 1970s mopeds. There is an established sports moped scene with specialist spares outlets, and restored and project bikes are regularly auctioned on the internet, where the market values of complete bikes and spare parts is now being set, and can be monitored.

Each model poses different spares problems, and as parts are getting harder to find, restorers are resorting to desperate measures. Chris Mahon once bought a whole bike for the exhaust pipe. Fantic Super T pipes are rare because they were cannibalised to make expansion chambers for other bikes, and the end pieces were prone to snapping off, so Chris bought a Fantic hybrid to get hold of a pristine pipe. Yamaha FS1-E rear mudguards are now so scarce people have bought complete FS1-Es to get a decent one.

"The Yamaha FS1-E is now much sought after, and people are always in wanting parts and second-hand stuff. They'll buy anything that can be straightened up and painted." - Terry Silvester

"I follow up any lead or contact whatsoever, and I'm a van driver so I can call in on old shops, or whatever. Sometimes the bike turns out to be half of one in a box so I've needed

Funky Mopeds

A typical garage find, Yamaha FS1-E. Some fresh fuel, and this timewarp special fired up willingly after languishing for 17 years in a garden shed.

... and this is now

Chris Mahon's unrestored Fantic TI. *"It's got character and authenticity, but it's a bit yucky."*

Funky Mopeds

FS1-E rear mudguards haven't stood the test of time.

to get two like that to make one." - Neil Holland.

"I've been all over the country for bikes and parts, and I drove for 28 hours to the south of Paris to get a Fantic Chopper, I found on the internet. I ended up making the Chopper up out of four bikes, it was the hardest bike I've done." - Steve Fitzsimmons.

"It frustrates me that parts are so scarce. It gets to me, and really winds me up when I could be so close to finishing, but can't do any more until I get that elusive part, and the bike's stuck, half-built in the shed. When that happens I go off and start another one, and the first one goes to the back of the queue. More and more parts are going to have to be made." - Neil Holland.

Mark Wilson admits to "... crafting a few bits and pieces ..." for his award winning Gitane Champion Veloce, and is using a rare fairing as a pattern to make reproductions for future restorations.

Paul Simcox manufactured a chainguard and an exhaust guard for a Fantic Chopper, later replacing them with genuine parts. "I've often made a part to use temporarily until the right bit comes along. I've never not found a part, even though it might take as long as three years to find it." said Paul.

Mark is struggling with his Gitanes and Testis. He said "I want to keep restoring them, but even though there are fewer parts than for FS1-Es, and there's not a lot to them, it's difficult to find the bits. Clocks are a real problem - I just can't find them. Brackets, rubbers, and back light lenses are also difficult to get."

John Dunn was able to buy parts from Steve Goode, a Puch specialist, for his Grand Prix, but was still stuck for a while. *"The hardest parts to find were the exhaust and footrests, but I tracked them down from a retired Devon Puch dealer who still had some parts."*

Gilera spares are relatively plentiful and mostly fairly cheap. Bob Wright of Bob Wright Motorcycles of Weston-Super-Mare, has brought Gilera spares back from Italy for many years.

"Gilera parts are easy to get' apart from Trials rear mudguards and chainguards, and adjustable Ceriani rear shockers." - Steve Wilkinson.

Barry Moore continues to advertise, and turns up bikes for restoration from time to time. *"There are still 'peds to be found, but I wouldn't want to do an FS1-E now. I would recommend anyone getting into moped restoration to tackle a Gilera. The engines don't usually have to be stripped. The crank seals are usually good."*

"FS1-E back mudguards and seats are the most difficult parts to get. Pattern parts are available, and they can be modified to be acceptable, but they're not as well made as the originals, and, of course, they're not authentic. I can tell them from 20 yards." - Charlie Owens.

Barry Moore agrees. *"It's mudguards, tanks and tank badges on FS1-Es, and swinging arms are the hardest parts to find for Suzuki AP50s. They rot. Seats and headlight shells are also difficult to find. Honda SS50 seats, pedal system parts and cranks can be difficult, but they're not a bad bike to do generally. There's a lot of pattern FS1-E switchgear around, without the tuning forks logo underneath, but genuine SS50 switchgear crops up a lot."*

"FS1-E pedal gear is hard to get because, unlike a lot of other parts on the bike, they weren't common to other models. Almost all the original mudguards have rotted away. You can get pattern guards, but you won't find a genuine mudguard, or exhaust, any more. Genuine rims are available, but they're expensive." - Russell Sears.

Brent Fielder has got five Garellis, but is restoring an early 4 speed Honda SS50; the actual bike owned by a friend when he and Brent were 16. *"I'm into Garellis!"* said Brent emphatically, *"But the Honda SS50 is a different animal,*

... and this is now

Italian moped engines. Clockwise from top left: Minarelli engines were supplied to many manufacturers including Fantic. Later compact system versions had aluminium barrels and a redesigned cylinder head. Gilera produced its own engines ... as did Garelli.

Funky Mopeds

and so well made by comparison. What would be a single component on a Garelli, can be broken down into many items on the Honda - it's more intricate. High quality stuff. Also, the wiring is a lot more complicated. There are no indicators, stop lights, or ignition switches on Garellis."

Paul Simcox has been restoring Garellis since 1991.

He said *"They're fairly simple. I've built all my own bikes, and I've helped maybe twenty others, but I was early on the scene, and it's getting more and more difficult to restore them. Garelli has been out of business since the 1980s, so there are no new parts. Tanks, for example, are just about impossible to get now."*

"Garelli mudguards are in short supply. They're not well supported, and they're prone to cracking under the seat. Rear suspension units are hard to find, and new seats are just about impossible, as are toolboxes for Tigers. It would cost about £1500 to do one, but all the parts are hoovered up now." - Brent Fielder.

Garellis were sold in large numbers in their home market, and elsewhere in Europe, but the continental bikes were of different specification. They had different barrels and carbs, exhausts, and even frames; there are so many differences very few have been brought into the UK.

There is, however, at least a certain degree of interchangeability of parts for the European bikes, which can be helpful. Cimattis have the same back lights as Testis and Gitanes, for example, Puch and Gitane brake parts are the same, and Minarelli engine parts are fairly plentiful. The

... and this is now

Italian manufacturers and UK importers often crossed over parts from one model to another. Malagutis were especially bad for this. The cycle parts were shipped separately to the engines and chassis, and the bikes were built up at the importer's premises in Ripley, Surrey. A lot of parts were interchangeable, and due to mix ups and shortages there was a great deal of inconsistency.

"Sometimes the wrong bits were slapped on at the factory, and there were hybrids, as models were changing over, and they were using up parts to shift stuff off the shelves. It sometimes leads to disputes about what's original." - Neil Holland.

"There are a lot of common parts that are interchangeable among bikes from the Italian manufacturers. Clocks, levers, even forks." - Chris Mahon

HARD EARNED SKILLS

Undertaking a motorcycle restoration may seem daunting to a newcomer, but not all successful restorers grew up learning mechanical skills from their fathers, or claim to have a natural aptitude for the work. Many are self-taught, and believe strongly that with patience and dedication, it would be possible for a beginner to emulate their achievements.

His father was a military despatch rider, so Brent Fielder has got motorcycling in the blood, so to speak, but he learned his mechanical and restoration skills on the job. "When I started, I was always rounding nuts off, and breaking, snapping, and bending things, but I got better. Through trial and error I gradually acquired some skills. My advice is to break the restoration down into distinct projects like forks, wheels, and engine, and have patience - you'll slowly get better at things. Mopeds are so simple I'd recommend anyone to do one, even if you think you're useless. It's just patience, and not stopping halfway through."

Julian Kowalewski is also largely self-taught. "I've learned as I've gone along, and nothing really frightens me now. My brother-in-law helped a bit. He didn't give me direct tuition, but he pointed me in the right direction and kept an eye on me, but I taught myself spraying and welding. It's very scary the first time you put paint in a gun and have a go, but that's exactly what you've got to do - have a go. Preparation is the key. It's an old cliché, but it's true."

"The hardest part comes once it's stripped down. Then there's no turning back." - John Dunn.

"The trick is to use the very best bits you can get hold of, and to restore the reusable parts you take apart the very best you can. When you're working up from the frame don't put anything on unless it's really good." - Brent Fielder.

"If I bolt something on, it stays on." agrees Neil Holland.

Mark Wilson: "Some people get their frames back, and put their bikes together with parts that aren't cleaned up, to see what they're going to look like. When I put a bike together, it stops together and doesn't come to bits again. I prefer to build up from the bottom, and wait for a part, if necessary."

Mark was a schoolboy motocrosser, and grew up working on bikes. "I've always been mechanically minded, and I've always had bikes. I'm one of three brothers and we were all successful at motocross, but it became too expensive."

"My granddad was a brilliant mechanic, and I watched him for hours when I was about 12 or 13. He taught me to adjust tappets, that sort of thing, and I've always messed around with cars. An old boy called Lionel, from a bicycle shop I used to go to taught me to rebuild wheels so I buy, or rechrome, the rims, and get a set of spokes, and build the moped wheels up myself. It takes anything between 20 minutes and two and a half hours to sort out the eggs, and buckles, and get them balanced and perfect." - Barry Moore.

"I've found good people for the paint, graphics, and the plating, and that's very important. Sometimes you send stuff off, and when it comes back it's not half what you were expecting. For example, there are a lot of bad chromers out there. Even though you're sending parts away for other people to work on, there's still a lot of hard work involved. It pays to clean stuff up the best you can to get the best possible results. It's obvious, but not everyone bothers." - Mark Wilson.

PARTNERS

When men are passionate about a hobby, their wives and girlfriends have to be patient and understanding. Spending cash that could pay for a new car or a holiday, on a box of rusty spares at an autojumble, staying out night after night, fettling a bike in the shed, and sitting at the computer until the early hours of the morning looking for parts and information on the internet, could put a strain on a relationship; thankfully most moped enthusiasts have partners more tolerant than most.

"She's given up. At one point, I had 36 'peds stuffed everywhere in the house as well as in the garage, the shed, and an outbuilding, and she still hasn't left me." - Barry Moore.

"Sue probably thinks we're just a lot of silly old men messing about, but she realises it's our hobby and interest, and she doesn't give me any grief." - Charlie Owens.

"She thinks it's great. We've met some lovely people." - Paul Simcox.

"My girlfriend's very tolerant about it. She finds it quite amusing. She knows I get a kick out of it, and I'm not in the pub, or the betting shop, or chasing women. She's happy for me to do something I enjoy. Life's a compromise, it's about give and take. The thing is not to take it to excess." - Brent Fielder.

Sometimes enthusiasts' other halves are not kept fully

Funky Mopeds

Restorers often find it hard to let go. Paul Simcox and Neil Holland have built up substantial collections.

in the picture. Chris Alty, a 50cc racer, remembers trying to find fairings for two lads out to recreate the FS1-E cafe racers they had when they were 16. "They could only come to see me at certain times because one of them hadn't told his wife what he was spending his time and money, on. She had no idea."

LETTING GO

Everything has its price, and restorers and collectors often find themselves receiving an offer they can't refuse for a machine they had no intention of selling. Barry Moore says people sometimes offer him silly money, or nag him, until he caves in, and there's no doubt there are buyers who just won't take no for an answer. There are other factors involved, including the need addicted restorers have to move on, and to always have a new and exciting project on the go.

Neil Holland is a case in point. "I've got everything I really want so I'll just show them and keep them, now." he said. "Unless something really special came up of course, and maybe two or three could be for sale at the right money."

Julian Kowalewski is more adamant about hanging on to his bikes. "It's a collection, there's nothing I intend selling."

It can be difficult to keep classic motorcycles in tip-top condition, and sometimes collections outgrow the storage space available. Damp conditions, for example, lead to rapid deterioration of chrome and aluminium finishes. Neil Holland: "You need a dry, warm place - in a shed, or damp garage, they deteriorate, and it's hard to keep on top."

"You can't just leave bikes in a shed because they'll deteriorate in a number of ways. They need regular attention, and if you're not careful the collection ends up owning you." - John Powell.

THE SPORTS MOPED OWNERS' CLUB

When a classic motorcycle magazine put a call out in 1995 for restorers and collectors of 1970s sports mopeds to get together for a photoshoot, it brought together a group of enthusiasts, who went on to form the Sports Moped Owners' Club.

The photographic session took place in Birmingham, and the resulting feature in *Classic Motorcycle Mechanics* magazine was successfully completed. The bikes' owners got on well, and at a follow up meeting in Swindon a year later Paul Simcox, Brent Fielder, Chris Alty, Chris Mahon, and his mate Gary got together in the pub and decided to get the club started.

"I borrowed a van from work, and took a Kreidler Florett, and a Testi Champion Special." remembered Chris Alty. "There were about 15 people there and a selection of bikes. Chris Mahon was wheelying his Fantic GT Super 6 in the pub car park, and it was a great day. I'd been inside the pub, and

was just coming back out when Paul Simcox asked me to be club secretary. It seemed I'd been voted in, in my absence. I said I'd give it a try. I got everyone's name and address, and that became the core of the club."

About 40 people joined in the first year, and numbers doubled the year after. Now there are more than 250 paid up members, and interest is growing all the time. Like all good clubs, it's a friendly network of contacts, and a wealth of pooled knowledge is available to members. The club's purpose, according to Chris, is simply to promote the use and restoration of sports mopeds.

"The club isn't promoted, but it's got a strong member base, and it's all about being a point of contact." said Chris. "If someone needs an answer to a technical question, or to find some spares, or get some advice, they can do it within the club."

Paul Simcox organises the club's stands at the bi-annual Stafford Shows. "It's brilliant and it's good fun. As well as being about the bikes, the club has provided a great social life, and I've met people worldwide. We all help each other, and there have been maybe only two or three people who I've had dealings with and realised 'he's in it for the money', but even they're nice blokes."

Barry Moore agrees. "The club's a good thing. In the club people help each other. Folk ring me a lot for spares and advice. It's nice to see new faces and to meet people with a common interest. I've got friends from all over the country from Bournemouth to Scotland."

Funky Mopeds

The 1970s classic motorcycle scene is growing all the time. Huge crowds attend the bi-annual Stafford Classic Shows.

"I've met people from all over the country and it's good fun. A good crack." - Mark Wilson.

Neil Holland and Julian Kowalewski from Herefordshire are long-time members. Neil said *"Julian and I went to the Stafford Show and saw the first SMOC stand. We'd seen Paul Simcox and the boys in the feature in* Classic Motorcycle Mechanics, *and it had boosted our enthusiasm even more."*

"Everyone in the club's helpful and friendly. We all help each other. Often we give each other stuff, and we don't even charge postage for sending it off." - Steve Fitzsimmons.

"We'll all put ourselves out for each other. I bought a bike, unseen, from the north of the country, and Barry Moore picked it up for me, looked after it, travelled 50 miles to someone else, who brought it down to me. I'd do the same for him." - John Powell.

It's not just about the bikes. The machines serve to bring people of a common age together, and, inevitably, they have more in common than sports mopeds. The music of the time is a big thing for a lot of people.

"Members who were 16 in the early sports moped years are sometimes big fans of glam rock. I know one guy who's got Jeepster by T-Rex on his answerphone message, whereas for me, punk was everything, and for others Northern Soul was the thing. The music was a massive part of life as a teenager, and the club puts people in touch to talk about it." - Chris Alty.

Many SMOC members have other 70s based and related hobbies. Chris Alty again *"I know quite a few are into Raleigh Choppers, and know them inside out. Frame numbers, colours,*

... and this is now

"The Tiger's got an old fashioned character but plenty of horsepower, even now." - Brent Fielder.

country lanes on a variety of 1970s 50cc machines. The events have settled into a fairly fixed calendar, starting with a get-together in Abergavenny on the second weekend in May, and ending with a run in Herefordshire in September.

"We all live far apart, but we get together two or three times a year, and it's a really enjoyable weekend. Typically we meet up for Saturday lunch in a pub and go for an afternoon ride. We hit the pubs on Saturday night and then we have another run out before Sunday lunch, and setting off for home." - Brent Fielder.

"I enjoyed fast bikes, in the 90s, but then I realised I could have just as much fun at half the speed. Riding these little bikes is great fun." - Paul Simcox.

"I had a Honda VFR, but I sold it, I didn't use it. I had more fun on the mopeds. It's b****y great going around on these little bikes. It brings back memories for everybody." - Neil Holland.

John Powell, a seventies Yamaha enthusiast, has a Honda Fireblade, but several times a year he takes his FS1-Es to a moped run. "It's probably the most dangerous riding I do." said John. "It's a load of 40-something-year-old men shamelessly reliving their youth, and no-one's fussed if anyone thinks it's sad."

John continued "My mate, Steve, got me started and we always have a good time. The people are a scream; a bunch of complete loonies. No, seriously, there are a lot of good people involved, and in fact it's the characters that make it so good, as much as the bikes. We take the bikes in vans and meet up in a pub car park at lunchtime. There's a lot of chat, it's a good way to find out stuff, and there's some parts swapping. Then there's a lot of racing in the afternoon and more of the same, the next day. It's all very tongue in cheek, but no-one wants to be beaten."

"It brings it all back. The smell of two-stroke oil. Our sides ache with laughing - I recommend it, it's a great laugh. I think I'll relax and enjoy the views, and if I'm at the back it doesn't

years of production, you name it."

The club is still run on the same lines as it was on the first day with Paul Simcox, and Chris Alty, and his wife, Paula at the hub. Contact Chris on 01695 720806 to become a member.

MOPED RUNS

Members of the Sports Moped Owners' Club meet up several times a year for a weekend of moped mayhem, hurtling around

Overleaf: Sports Moped Owners' Club members meet up several times a year, ending with a get-together in Hereford in September.

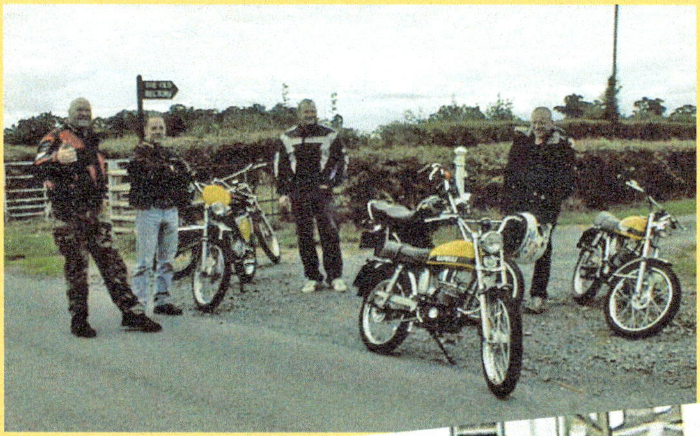

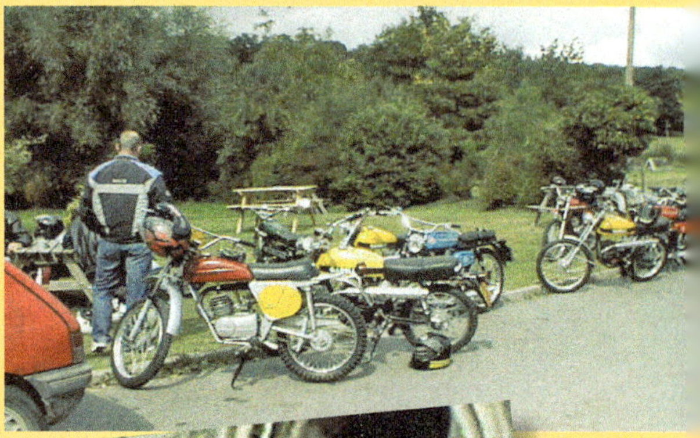

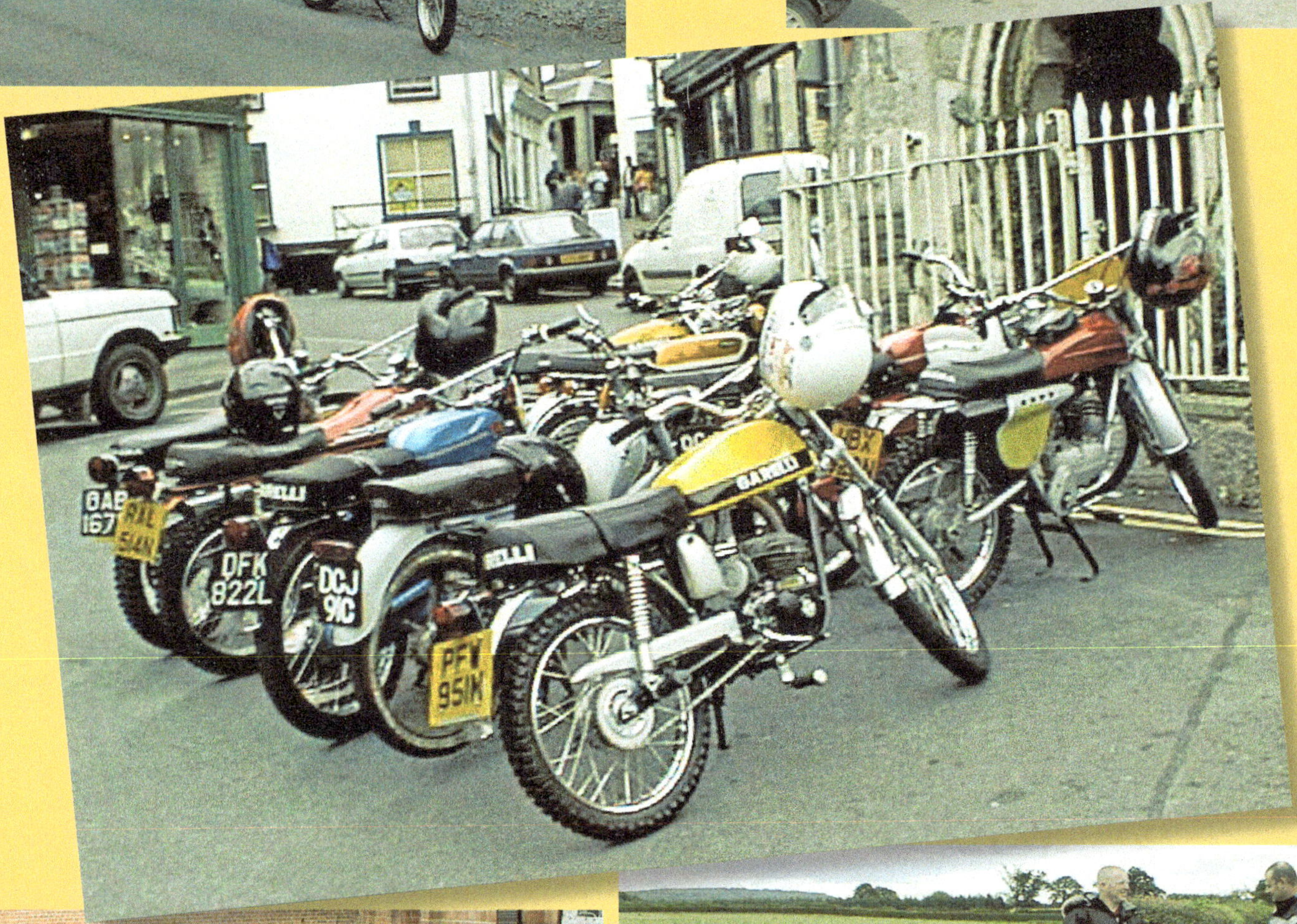
GARELLI
DFK
822L
DCJ
91C
PFW
951K

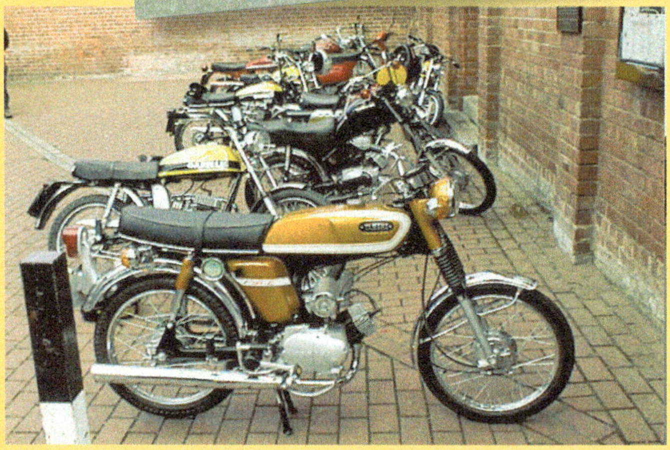

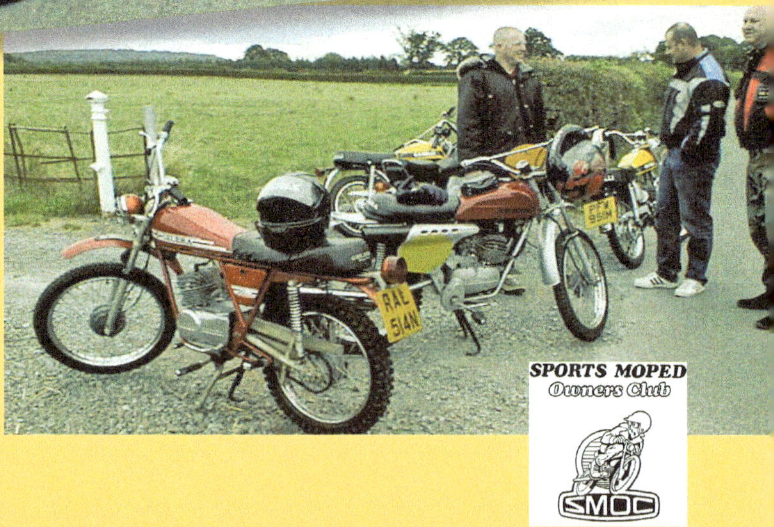

SPORTS MOPED
Owners Club
SMOC

... and this is now

Paul Simcox and son set off on their Garellis. (Courtesy Paul Simcox)

matter, but then one'll come by caning it a bit. Before long, we're all on the tank, racing." - Barry Moore.

"It's great fun. Nobody has to beat anybody else, but we get a bit carried away. We start off going for a gentle ride, and before we know it everyone's going flat out. It's nuts really, we're mostly on mint bikes, and I'm holding it wide open thinking 'It's going to blow, it's going to blow!'" - Brent Fielder.

Chris Alty is a regular competitor in 50cc racing at circuits up and down the country throughout the summer. His racing commitments keep him away from his family a great deal so he has only attended one moped run, but it left an indelible mark on his memory.

"It was exactly like riding mopeds was years ago." said Chris, "Fiercely competitive and people falling off. There was a guy with a beautiful Casal Phantom 5, but there was something very wrong with the front brake, the brake plate wasn't anchored properly, or something, and the front wheel locked solid, and threw him off the bike. The bike was bashed up and he cut his forearms open.

"Then we stopped at one point, and the guy at the back of the group, on an SS50, had disappeared." continued Chris. "It turned out he'd crashed trying to keep up. Someone cruelly said it was the shock of seeing 40mph on the speedo! Speed's the thing you see. Everybody still wants to have the fastest bike."

"It's ultra competitive, and a lot of the FS1-Es on the runs have got 65cc barrels, and some of the Garellis have got 70cc kits." - Brent Fielder.

"I enjoy club runs very much provided all the bikes are actually 49cc and we're all on a level playing field. A lot of the bikes are oversized and tuned up. It's incredibly competitive. You can be a quarter of an hour trying to pass someone, lying on the tank." - Julian Kowalewski.

Funky Mopeds

John Powell is less of a purist in this respect. *"Originality matters less than being the fastest. The bikes I take on runs are different to my show bikes. Steve and I take two bikes each in case one blows up because we absolutely cane the things, wringing their necks for 100 miles or so. It's a real laugh, and I'll continue to make an effort to stay involved"*

"Andy Carter is a top drag racer and a record holder at Santa Pod. I'm tuning his Fantic Super T so when he goes with the club on runs, he won't be left at the back. That's how serious it is!" - Chris Alty.

Creator of the Yamaha FS1-E website, Russell Sears uses his restored candy orange machine for occasional fair weather rides, and is impressed by the bike's all-round capability and modern feel. *"It's fantastic. It's smooth, and revvy, and rides really well, and it doesn't feel like an old bike at all. It's definitely still got it."*

"You only live once. These bikes are going to be around long after we've gone so we might as well use them while we can. If you don't think you'd have enough power you'd be well off the mark. Just stay off the main roads, and they're fantastic fun. The Tiger's got an old fashioned character, but plenty of horsepower, even now." - Brent Fielder.

"It's good to show the bikes off. On runs we always stop at bikers' haunts, and when we do, no-one's interested in the Fireblades and R1s, they just swarm around the 'peds." - Barry Moore.

BARRY MOORE'S RESTORATION CHECKLIST

Moped addict, Barry Moore, casts an eye over a typical 'garage find' Gilera Trials, and comes up with a list of pointers for would-be restorers.

- Find the best bit of unfaded original colour, and use it as a colour match for respraying (eg inside side panels).
- Sandblast the frame and tinware.
- Repaint all the above.
- Blast the airbox, and repaint in black.
- Get the fork stanchions and shock damping rod hard chromed.
- Remove all the spokes, and shotblast them, clean them up with a wire wheel or replace with new sets.

- Check the engine – it's fairly bulletproof and, with any luck, shouldn't need any work.
- Strip the bike completely.

- Rechrome the bars, pedal cranks, and wheel rims (they're often rotten and not worth salvaging, but are OK in this case).
- Also rechrome the shock springs and the gear lever.

Funky Mopeds

- Replace most of the screws throughout the bike.
- Rebuild and balance the wheels.
- Put the original tyres back onto the rims.
- Replace the missing exhaust and speedometer with 'new old stock' or refurbished second-hand parts.
- Fit a new set of cables.
- Apply replacement tank and sidepanel stickers, and brand stickers for the fork bottoms and shock absorbers.
- Fit new old stock replacement grips.
- Purchase, and fit, a new headlight rim.

- Glass bead blast the engine casings (this method doesn't damage the aluminium).
- Polish the outer engine casings, wheel hubs, and brake plates.
- Rebuild the engine with a new set of Allen screws.
- Zinc plate the wheel spindles, swinging arm spindle, and all salvageable nuts, bolts, and brackets.

- Replace the headlight switch with good second-hand part.
- Check the wiring - it appears sound at this stage.
- Sandblast, and powdercoat, the seat base.
- Fit a new cover on the original seat foam.
- Clean the tops and bottoms of the shocks with a wire wheel, and repaint.
- Fit a new rear light lens.

... and this is now

- Sandblast, and repaint, the mudguards.
- Refit the mudguards using replacement nuts and bolts.
- Polish the levers.
- Purchase, and fit, a new chrome cover for the throttle assembly.
- Replace the cylinder head with a second-hand part (this one has a broken fin).

- Clean the headlight brackets, top and bottom yokes, and fork bottoms to the bare aluminium, and repaint in silver.
- Fit new pedals.
- Fit a new steering lock.
- Fit a new petrol cap.
- Strip the carburettor, clean it with petrol and a toothbrush, and reassemble.

www.veloce.co.uk
Details of all Veloce books • New book news • Special offers • Newsletter

CHAPTER FIVE
GALLERY

The competition yellow Yamaha FS1-E DX was painted in the styl of Kenny Roberts' works Yamaha racers.

Gallery

The Yamaha FS1-E DX in its natural suburban habitat.

Funky Mopeds

Julian Kowalewski restored this Fantic TI after finding it in a skip. "The owner was throwing it away but as soon as I asked if I could have it he demanded £70 for it. We eventually settled on £30."

Gallery

Gilera 50 Touring. A sturdy and sensible sports moped.

Funky Mopeds

Fantic Caballero. This actual machine featured in a *Bike* magazine road test in July 1976.

Above: KTM Comet Cross.

Gilera Trials and Touring. The Trials lay under a Welsh farm hedge for 20 years before being restored. Now it's certified by the Gilera factory as a 100 per cent correct restoration.

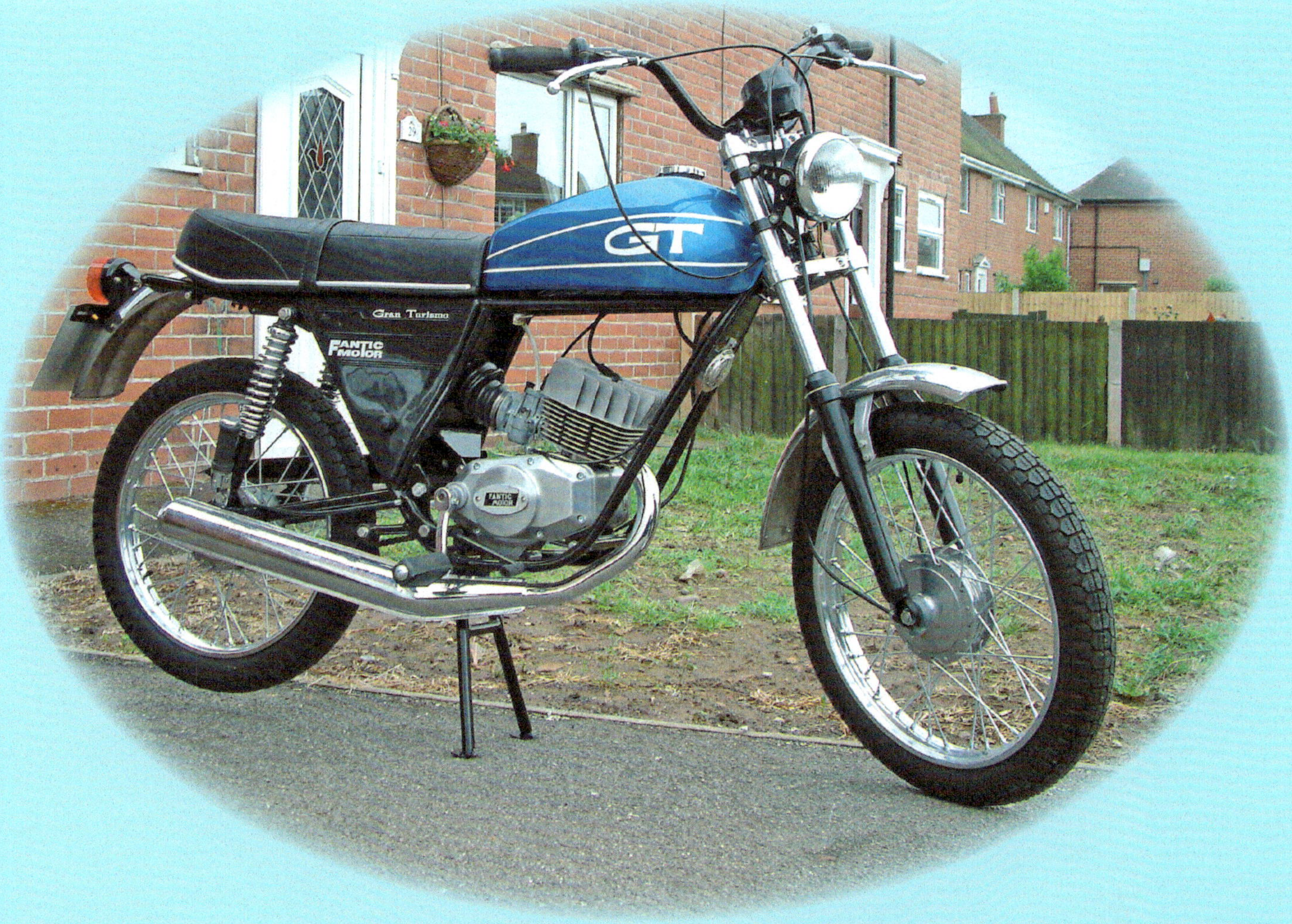
GT
Gran Turismo
FANTIC MOTOR

Fantic GT. Part of the second generation of Fantic sports mopeds.

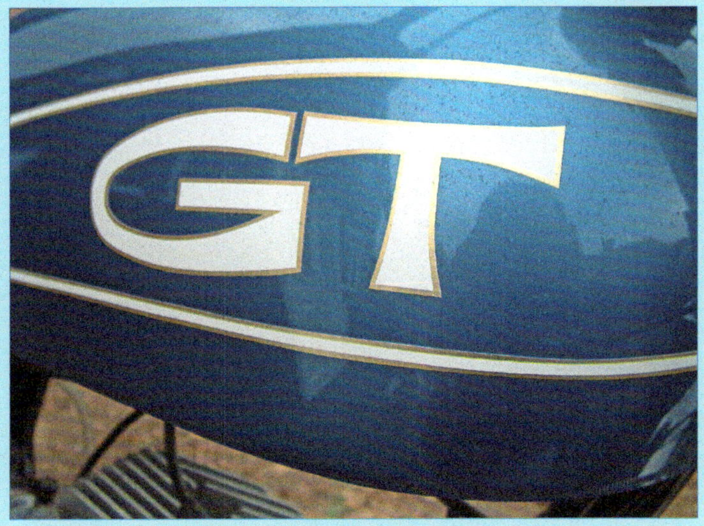
GT

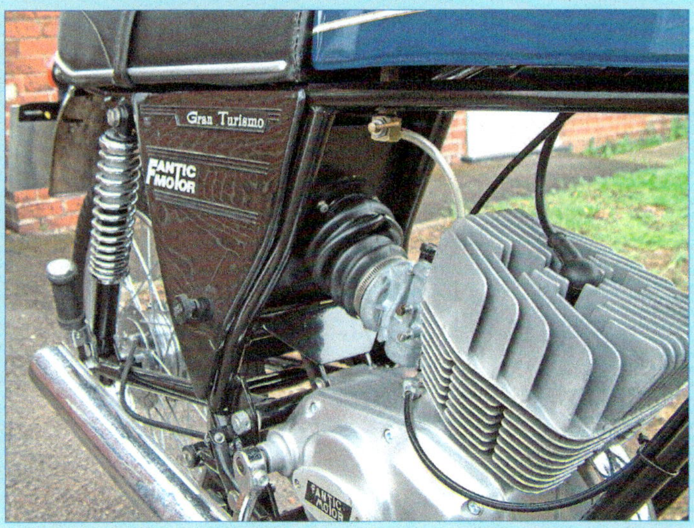
Gran Turismo
FANTIC MOTOR

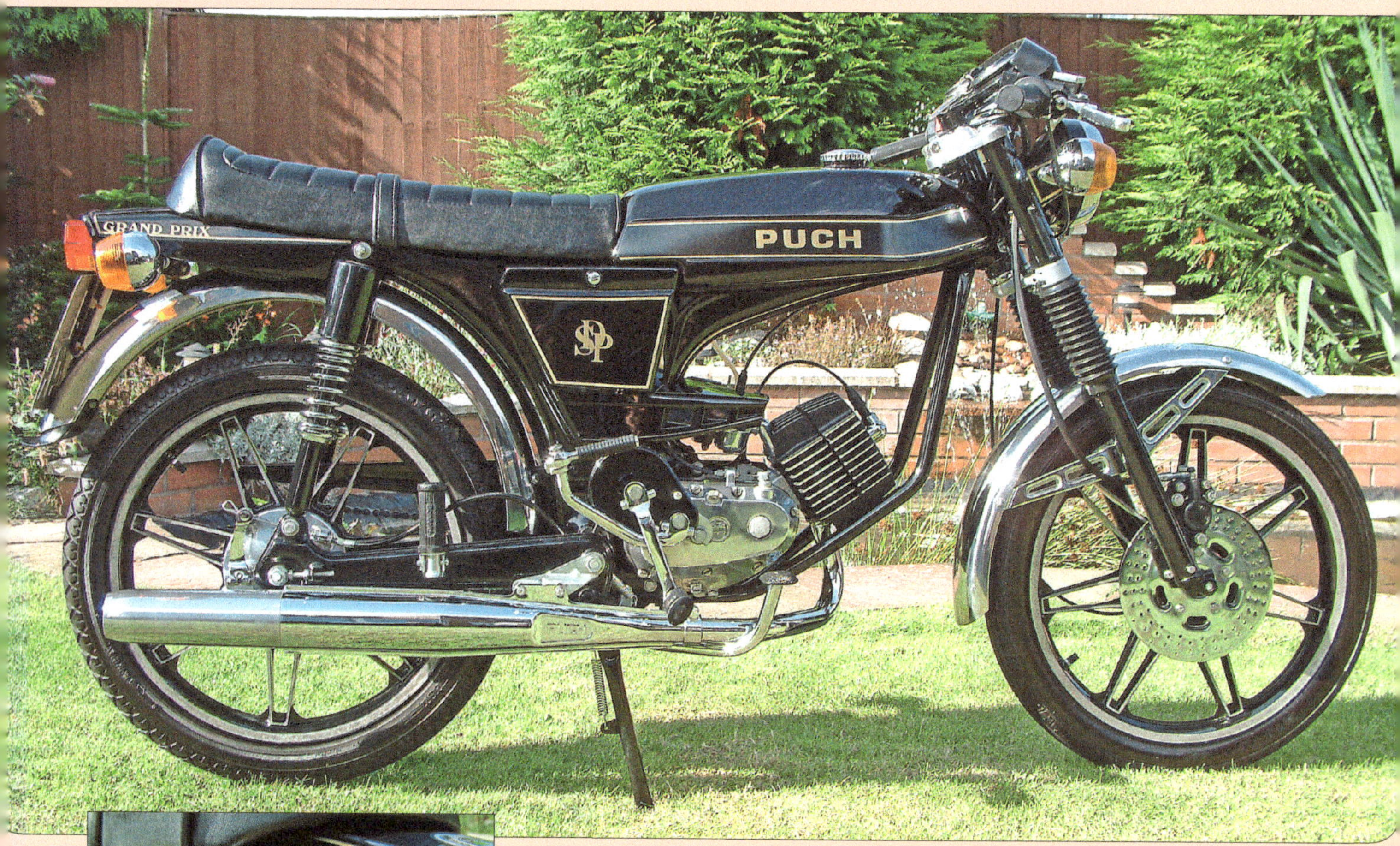
GRAND PRIX
PUCH

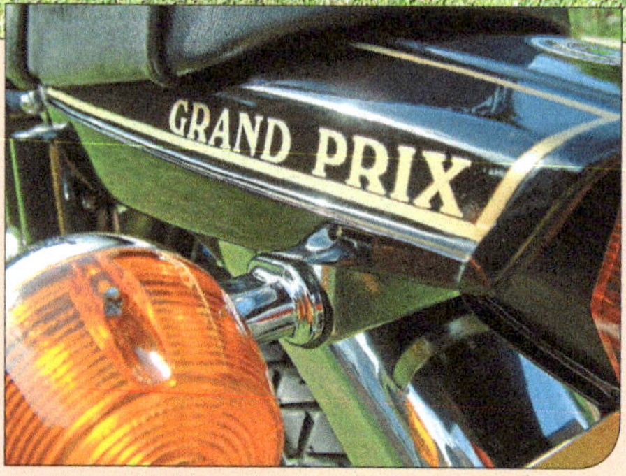
GRAND PRIX

John Dunn's award winning Puch Grand Prix Supreme is finished to a higher standard than the original bike. Improved parts include generally superior paintwork and polished surfaces, downtubes (not on the original bike), brake switch, drilled disc, and rubber brake pedal cover.

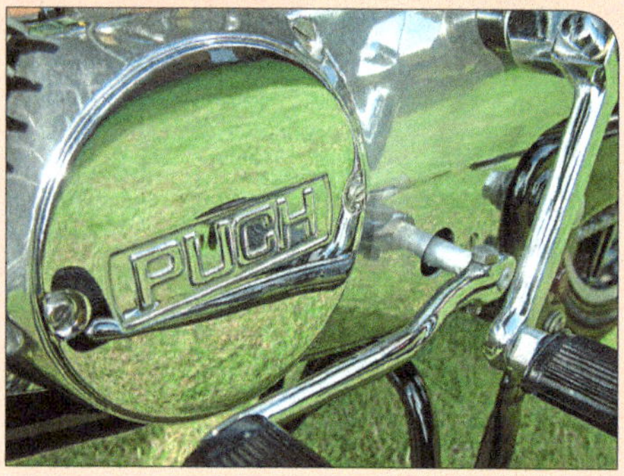
PUCH

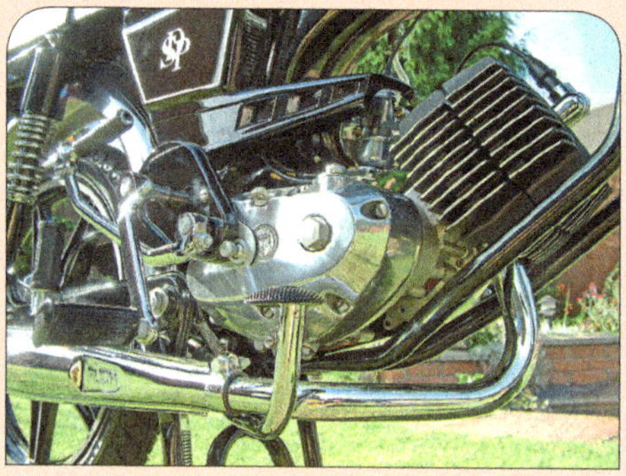

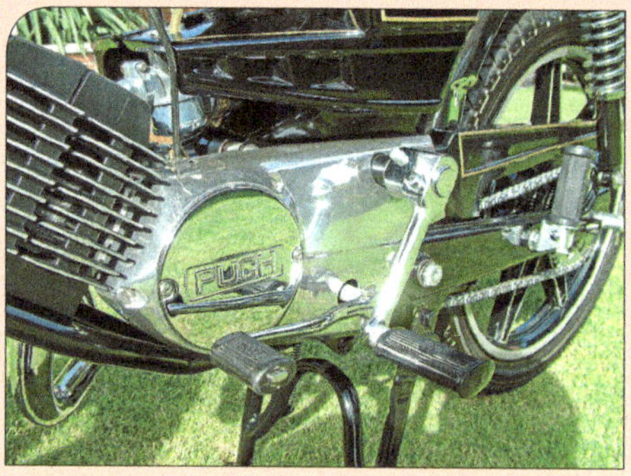
PUCH

Gallery

Mark Wilson's triple award winning Gitane Champion Veloce was bought for £200 after weeks of haggling. It had bent forks, a smashed wheel, and its fibreglass was damaged, but it was complete apart from its coil, magneto flywheel, and carburettor. A lot of hard work turned it into this rare and exquisite restoration.

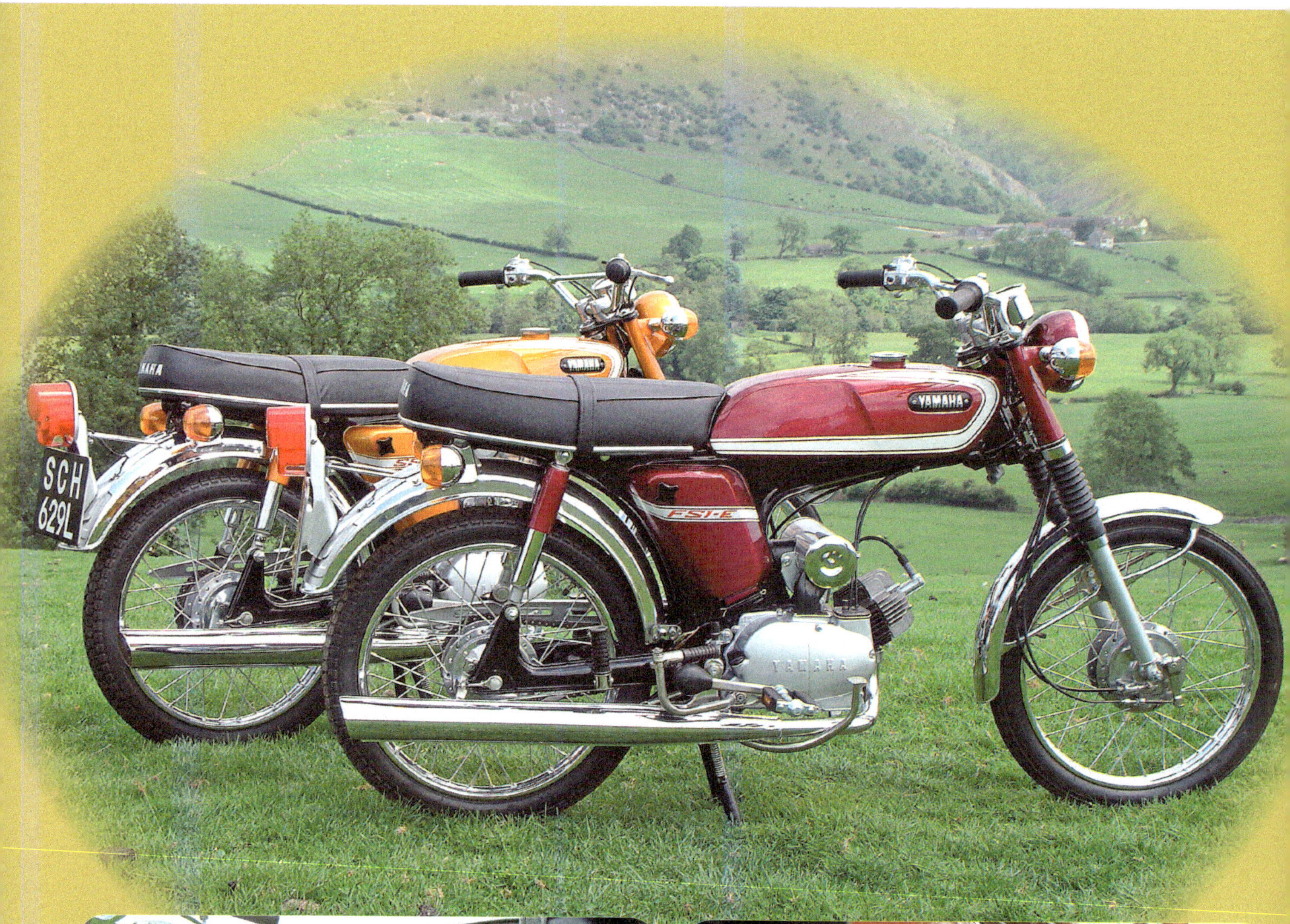
YAMAHA
SCH
629L
FSI-E

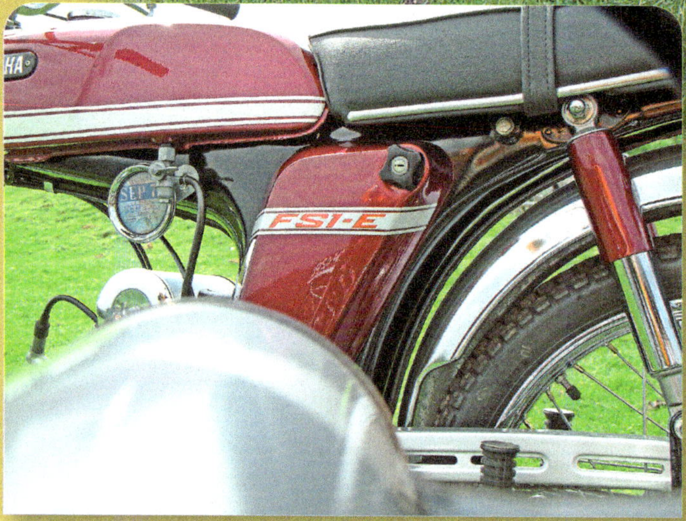
FSI-E

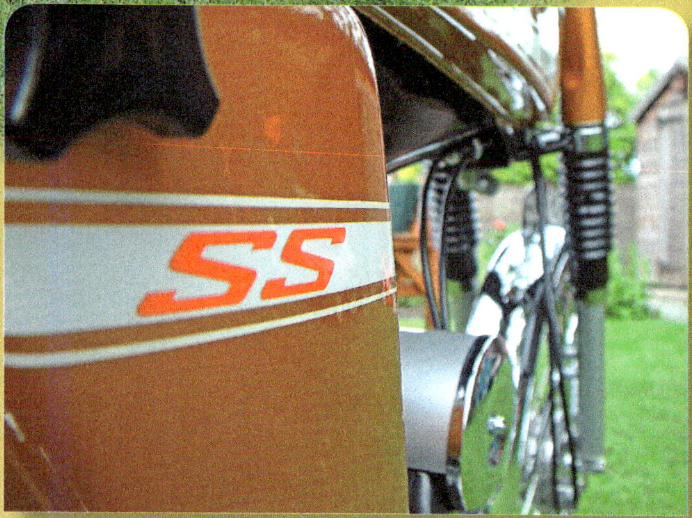
SS

Gallery

Charlie Owens's FS1-Es stand out from other restored fizzies by virtue of their completely original paintwork.

Funky Mopeds

The monoshock Gitane Champion Veloce was an advanced motorcycle in its day.

Gallery

Paul Simcox rebuilt this Malaguti Cavolcone Cross using all 'new old stock' parts. Consequently, it's effectively a brand new bike.

Funky Mopeds

The five speed Suzuki AP50 was a marginally better motorcycle than the Yamaha FS1-E.

Gallery

1973 Candy orange SS-badged FS1-Es are the most sought after Yamaha sports mopeds. SS stood for 'sixteener special'.

The Fantic Caballero arrived in the UK in August 1974.

Funky Mopeds

Yamaha FS1-E tank badges have been known to fetch £80 a pair on eBay!

Puch Grand Prix Supreme.

Motorcycles in the 1970s were usually painted in cheerful colours, and sports mopeds were no exception.

KTM built successful motocross machines, but their sports mopeds weren't big sellers.

The matt black tank of a Garelli Tiger Special.

Malaguti sold a range of sports mopeds throughout the sports moped era.

Gallery

A pair of Gileras.

Funky Mopeds

The Malaguti Superquattro, forerunner of the Olympique.

Gallery

Garelli Rekord Mk II and early Gilera Touring.

CHAPTER SIX
THE FABULOUS FS1-E

As much a seventies icon as the Space Hopper and the Raleigh Chopper, the Yamaha FS1-E is a landmark machine with its own web site, and is a true classic. It was by far the biggest selling 1970s sports moped, and was voted the seventh best motorcycle of all time by readers of *Bike* magazine in 2003. The fantastic 'fizzy' stirs up more memories than any other bike in its class, having given tens of thousands of sixteeners their first taste of vehicular independence and freedom.

The Yamaha FS1 model was first available in Holland

The FS1-E arrived in the UK in January 1973.

in 1970, and the manufacture of British market FS1-Es is believed to have begun in Japan on 5 November 1972. Those first machines arrived at UK dealers in January 1973, and the model was an instant best seller, remaining so until the end of the sports moped era. The fizzy was then available in Britain, on and off, in restricted form and without pedals, until the late 1980s.

Yamaha first established links with the Dutch motorcycle trade in 1960, and started exporting to the Netherlands soon afterwards. In 1968, the Japanese concern decided to create a subsidiary company in Holland, and Yamaha NV, in Amsterdam, became its European HQ.

Although hugely popular all over Europe, the moped was a strange concept to the Japanese, and there was none in the Yamaha line-up in the late 1960s. However, the European moped market was too big to ignore, and the Dutch looked at the Yamaha range to find a model suitable for conversion. The F5B, which had a pressed steel frame and a 50cc rotary induction engine, was considered and rejected, and the FS1, under development in Japan in 1969, was chosen instead.

Henk Dullens, service manager of the Motorpaleis motorcycle shop, designed a pedal system that would meet Dutch laws. Moreover, it could be fitted to the production model with a minimum of changes, and photographs and drawings were sent, via Yamaha NV, to the Japanese factory. Pedal assemblies were manufactured in Japan, and the pedals themselves were added at Yamaha NV in Holland. The Dullens system was not patented, and other Japanese factories were later to produce similar designs.

The converted FS1 was put on the market in Holland at the beginning of 1970. The engines were detuned for Dutch market (90kph down to 40kph), and used the FB5 cylinder. The FS1's high level exhaust was replaced by the low level FB5 system, the timing was altered, and a 10mm carburettor replaced the standard 16mm unit. The bike was available in candy orange or candy blue. For the first year only, the frames were sprayed the same colour as the bodywork; thereafter, they were painted black. The hybrid bike was a big success, and 6500 machines were sold in the first year, and 8000 in 1971. This accounted for half of Yamaha's total European sales. The FS1 continued to be available in Holland until 1983.

According to legend, British dealer, Fowlers of Bristol, was enthusiastic about the FS1 after seeing a Dutch brochure, and the interest led to the creation of the British specification FS1-E. Yamaha UK was initially irked, as it had no plans to import the model, but this was soon forgotten as the bike became an immediate best seller in Great Britain. Within three months of introduction, it was Yamaha UK's best selling model.

So, what is it about the Yamaha FS1-E that made it such a success? Essentially, it is a simple, small motorcycle with

The fabulous FS1-E

Yamaha technical publications. The parts list shows clearly that the E of FS1-E stands for England.

17inch wheels built around a pressed steel spine frame, powered by a 49cc disc valve two-stroke engine, which produces 4.8bhp at 7000rpm in standard tune. It's strong, well engineered, and smooth, and comfortable on the road: furthermore, it's an attractive bike, with timeless styling that still looks fresh after more than thirty years.

Above all else, it's the FS1-E's character that has won it so many admirers. Friendly, and fun to ride, reliable, nippy, willing, and tireless, the little Yamaha is fondly remembered by many thousands who rode them in the seventies, and it also won fans in the motorcycle trade.

Terry Silvester, a Yamaha dealer, sold 40 gold SS FS1-Es in 1973: *"The FS1-E was the right bike at the right time. It was affordable, and light, and manoeuvrable, and not overpowered. It was a sensible starting point for youngsters, and it sold really well. We were selling a lot of two-stroke Yamahas at the time, but I would guess the FS1-E was responsible for approximately half our sales that year."*

"Yamaha were in on the act, early, and it was an appealing product at the right money. It was cheaper than Garellis and Fantics, and far more reliable, and just looked so good." - Charlie Owens

"It was one of the best selling Yamahas, ever. They were fast, and they were hardy, and they never broke. It was a great package for kids leaving school. We would take as many as Yamaha could supply. We couldn't get enough

Yamaha magazine advertisement from August 1974.

89

Funky Mopeds

Exciting things happen when you ride a Yamaha FS1-E DX.

of them. We took them in lorry loads and they were always gone straightaway. People had to wait for the next batch." - Peter Padgett.

"Yamaha must've made a lot of money out of the FS1-E. They were big sellers, and the profits must have helped them develop their range. It must've helped them immensely in other ways, too. People developed an affection for Yamahas and bought bigger bikes from them." - Russell Marsden.

"The FS1-E was a variation of a bike that had been available in other markets since the sixties, and it didn't cost a lot for Yamaha to develop and build them. The FS1-E helped establish Yamaha in the UK." - Charlie Owens.

"Yamaha were already well and truly on the map, but the FS1-E generated a lot of sales, and created a lot of loyal customers. People became addicted to Yamahas because of it." - Peter Padgett.

"Garellis were faster because of their chrome barrel, but they would seize up, and you'd have to push them home, then you could be off the road for months, waiting for spares. With the FS1-E, you could go to your Yamaha dealer and if they didn't have the parts already, they'd come through in three or four days." - Russell Marsden.

"Yamaha was always a good company for spares." - Terry Silvester.

"The FS1-E was very reliable, but there were crashes, and the oils weren't as good as they are today. There was a huge spares market and we sent parts by mail order all over the country, and we supplied parts abroad, even to Holland. We used to order pedal cranks 500 at a time, we'd order pistons in 500s, or even 1000 at a time, and we sold hundreds of tyres. Lead time was a factor, as we had to make sure we had everything in stock at all times to offer a first class service, but even so, we just don't place orders anything like that any more. It was phenomenal." - Peter Padgett.

"The FS1-E was tough and well made, but it wasn't really developed. It remained pretty static throughout its life. There was a disc brake model, but it was a gimmick and the bike didn't need it. Sales tapered off throughout the seventies as there was more competition, and a second hand market was generated, but it remained a strong seller to the end." - Terry Silvester.

"The simplicity of the moped was part of its appeal. It was a simple little bike. I wish I had a thousand of them, right now." - Peter Padgett.

FS1-E chronology

L reg (1 August 1972 to 31 July 1973)
SS (sixteener special) stickered candy orange FS1-Es were available in the UK, from January '73 onwards. Honda objected to Yamaha using SS side panel stickers as it already had an established SS model.

M reg (1 August 1973 to 31 July 1974)
A handful of orange SS bikes were sold on M plates, otherwise all M registered machines were released with FS1-E side panel stickers.

Popsicle purple and candy orange bikes with FS1-E side panel stickers sold side-by-side through the registration year.

(The M reg SS bikes were an oddity, perhaps due to a late delivery, or big shipment, just before the registration change. It would be unlikely to be because they were unsold machines stuck in showrooms, as the dealers were selling FS1-Es as fast as they could get them.)

N reg (1 August 1974 to 31 July 1975)
Candy orange FS1-Es were now no longer available or extremely rare.

The fabulous FS1-E

Candy orange SS badged FS1-Es went on sale in January 1973.

Popsical purple FS1-Es became available during the M registration year.

The FS1-D had its ignition switch moved from the left side panel to beside the speedometer.

Competition yellow drum braked FS1-Es were sold for a short period at the beginning of the P registration year. (August 1975.)

Popsicle purple bikes were sold throughout the N registration year.

Baja brown FS1-Es were introduced.

By 1975 just popsicle purple, and baja brown bikes were being sold.

P reg (1 August 1975 to 31 July 1976)

The final registration year for popsicle purple bikes.

Baja brown FS1-Es continued to be sold.

In August 1975, for one month only, a competition yellow drum braked FS1-E was sold. Apart from their paint colour, these bikes were identical to previous UK machines, and used the same tanks with white stripes, and screw-on badges.

Subsequently, the first fizzy with a front disc brake was released, the FS1-D. Also in competition yellow, this model again used the established badged tank with white stripes. The ignition switch was moved from the left side panel and positioned next to the speedometer.

Later in the P registration year the FS1-E, and new FS1-E D, were given a makeover resulting in a number of cosmetic changes. The new bikes were given a smooth sided tank without screw-on badges. Renamed the FS1-E DX, the disc braked version continued to be supplied in competition yellow, and the drum braked FS1-E was sold in baja brown. Both models featured a black and white speed blocks design on their tanks, and side panels in the style of Kenny Roberts's TZ Yamaha racing bikes.

R reg (1 August 1976 to 31 July 1977)

The second, and final, registration year for the new competition yellow FS1-E DXs, and baja brown FS1-Es.

During this year, the redesigned FS1 autolube model with plastic side panels became available. The disc brake model was usually sold in chappy red, and the drum brake version was normally supplied in space blue. The pedal arrangement was retained, but spinning footrest style blocks replaced the bicycle type pedals on the ends of the pedal arms.

S reg (1 August 1977 to 31 July 1978)

FS1s continued in restricted form as the FS1E-A and FS1E-DXA. The pedal shaft and pedalling system was replaced by a footrest bar. The left hand engine cover was redesigned, and holes in the swinging arm were capped off with blanking grommets.

Thereafter the FS1-E continued in various guises, including a chopper variant, and was around until about 1983. It then returned four years later, making a comeback as the FS1M. These bikes were made by the MBK factory in France, which had been taken over by Yamaha.

Funky Mopeds

The 1975 FS1-D disc brake model.

The standard drum braked FS1-E continued to be manufactured throughout 1975, but in baja brown. (Artist: Matt Chambers)

A 1976 FS1-E in baja brown. The colour is named after the famous desert races held on the Baja Peninsula in Southern California, in which Yamaha enjoyed considerable success.

The FS1-E DX sporting its 'Kenny Roberts stripes', aka 'racing ladders' or 'speed blocks'.

The FS1 featured Yamaha's autolube system, doing away with the need to mix oil and petrol in the fuel tank.

Restricted FS1DX with footpegs replacing the pedals.

The drum brake option continued as the FS1.

The fabulous FS1-E

The Yamaha Rebel, a chopper version of the FS1-E, was sold in the 1980s.

1980s FS1Ms made the fizzy popular all over again.

Fizzy Galore

Huddersfield bike breaker Russell Marsden, and his wife Margaret, detected an increase in interest in the Yamaha FS1-E, in 1999. Anticipating the FS1-E boom that took place over the next few years, they founded the specialist parts, and services business, Fizzy Galore. For several years now, the couple have made their living from the FS1-E, and have had a central role in the sports moped revival movement. Above all, though, Russell and Margaret are enthusiasts, who can trace their involvement with the model back to the FS1-Es they owned and rode in the mid-1970s.

"I do it for the fun of it, and I'm interested in fizzies myself, it's not as if I never had one." said Russell. "I'm not just in it for the money, I'm a part-creator of the fizzy boom and I like to think I'm doing something worthwhile. It is a business, but I'm providing a service supplying genuine and pattern parts, and I'm also happy to offer help and advice."

The level of interest in FS1-Es has turned out to be greater than Russell expected. I didn't know there were so many as have turned up." said Russell. "I've got over 1000 customers, and some have got two or three bikes, or more, up to nine bikes, even."

Who are Russell and Margaret's customers, and what do they do with their bikes? "Ninety-five per cent of people with a fizzy today had one when they were 16, and most of them keep it in good condition, and run it in good weather

Margaret Marsden at the Fizzy Galore stand at a classic motorcycle show. Outside Fizzy Galore's Huddersfield headquarters.

Funky Mopeds

for old times' sake." Russell explained. *"The other five per cent? Perhaps they had a Honda SS50, but the FS1-E was the bike they always wanted. Maybe it was their mates, who had FS1-Es, and they rode one and wished they had one, too."*

Fizzy Galore sells a huge range of parts, and offers a number of services such as exchange paintwork sets and seat recovering. As well as supplying hundreds of essential mechanical and electrical parts, the company stocks all the hard to get screws, washers, and rubber grommets, and caps needed to complete a restoration.

Russell comments *"FS1-Es are pampered now, and the owners look after them. People buy all the fiddly little bits that nobody bothered with in the seventies, and they spend time cleaning, and polishing, and perfecting them. Imperfect or dinged bits have to be replaced these days, but we used to keep riding them with a broken clutch ball end, or a broken speedo cable, or whatever, and as long as they kept going, we rode on for months. The air filter element is a best selling part, which amuses me as nobody ever changed them in the seventies. We'd run the bikes without rather than buy a new one. Perhaps people buy them now because they owed them to their original fizzies!"*

Knowledgeable about all things FS1-E, Russell has become established as one of the country's leading fizzy experts, and judges the FS1-E awards at the annual Vintage Japanese Motorcycle Show, at Lotherton Hall near Leeds. *"I know a lot, but I'm still picking things up and learning all the time. I've got an eye for originality, and I can pick out certain bits that are wrong, usually parts from later bikes that have been put on earlier ones."*

A line-up of fizzies at the Vintage Japanese Motorcycle Club show at Lotherton Hall, near Leeds.

Some FS1-E parts have become virtually impossible to find, and Fizzy Galore is addressing the problem by getting some components remanufactured. Russell said *"I'm looking into having some parts manufactured, including pattern mudguards, with all the holes in the right places, and chromed rear light stays. I'm also getting pedal change over forks, and some springs, made to order. There's more I'd like to do, rear light towers for instance, but they're too expensive to tool up for. It's not worth it, unfortunately."*

Russell is planning for Fizzy Galore to be around for the foreseeable future, but has some concerns about the spiralling values of the FS1-E and the cost of some spares. Prices and values are being set on internet auction site, eBay, and ever increasing activity on the site is driving the market upwards. *"I still think there are some undiscovered fizzies out there, and as long as bikes are being found and restored, we'll carry on, but it's different now from a few years ago, there's an awareness that fizzies are desirable and collected, and it's getting more expensive to buy and restore them. The cost of doing them up is getting too much, and I'm worried it'll get so dear that people won't do it."*

The FS1-E on eBay

The internet auction site, eBay, has become the main market place for buying and selling FS1-Es with several hundred items being sold at any one time, including complete restored and unrestored machines. But *caveat emptor!* All is not necessarily what it seems, and there are a number of dangers for the less knowledgeable.

"Bikes circulate. People get in on the craze and collect, then they realise they've got too much, and sell some off or they decide to specialise. Others are just selling spare bits to fund their hobby. That's all OK, but there are people out there kidding a lot of folk. They buy and sell FS1-Es, cobbling bikes together, and swapping parts about, and newcomers get caught out." - Russell Marsden.

People buy a totally wrecked 1970s FS1-E, or sometimes just a frame and log book, and then they build the bike back up using parts from 1980s models.

There are also a great number of supposedly difficult to find parts sold on eBay that are, in fact, still available from Yamaha dealers and specialists like Fizzy Galore. These new parts are bought by traders, and drip fed onto the auction site. Marketed as rare unused FS1-E parts, they regularly fetch many times their normal retail price. Some sellers source their new spares in Holland, where the bike was originally sold in FS1 form. Again, there is no need for restorers to bid against each other for them as they are available, at the prices the traders are paying, to anyone with access to the internet, or even simply by telephone. Finally, there are also a lot of

The fabulous FS1-E

pattern items around, such as mudguards and exhausts, and these are sometimes sold as genuine Yamaha parts. Even if the seller is clear the parts are not original spares, some items are of extremely poor quality and appearance, and even the best usually need modifying to look correct and to fit properly on a bike.

www.fs1e.co.uk

Russell Sears, a fizzy fanatic, started an FS1-E website in 2002, and was amazed how much interest it attracted. Now the site is at the centre of the FS1-E revival movement, having received more than 154,000 hits in its first two years.

"I've always had a fascination for the fizzy," explained Russell, "I had one and sold it when I was 17, and regretted it for years afterwards. There was a period of about 20 years when I never even saw one, but it never really left my mind. Then, when I was about 40 I got into classic bikes, and at the Stafford classic bike show one year, I stumbled across a restored fizzy on a stand. I stood and looked at it for an hour, and decided what I was going to do was restore one, too."

Spurred on, Russell traced and completely rebuilt the candy orange FS1-E he had when he was 16, meticulously building the bike up using correct and genuine Yamaha parts. Then, having catalogued the restoration and kept a comprehensive photographic record, he decided to post the story on the internet.

"When I restored mine, I found it difficult to get some of the information I needed. I was alone in many ways, so I decided to see what interest there was in what I was doing. I bought the fs1e.co.uk domain name and set up the site, and was immediately inundated by e-mails. The reaction was phenomenal."

The site is now the focal point for fizzy enthusiasts, with both fun and factual sections, an active shop, and busy message boards for enthusiasts to swap ideas and information. There is a members' section carrying information about the best places to buy spares and how much to pay, the site's mailing list is more than 800 strong, and there are more than 600 machines on Russell's official FS1-E register, bikes that are actually in existence with recorded frame, engine, and registration numbers.

FS1-E values have increased dramatically, since Russell restored his gold SS model in 2001, and, like most people involved with classic motorcycles, he is at a loss to explain the phenomenon completely. "The most sought after ones are the early gold, and purple, and baja brown bikes. They fetch huge money, and the top price in 2004 was £3000. It reflects their rarity value, how hard they are to restore, the cost

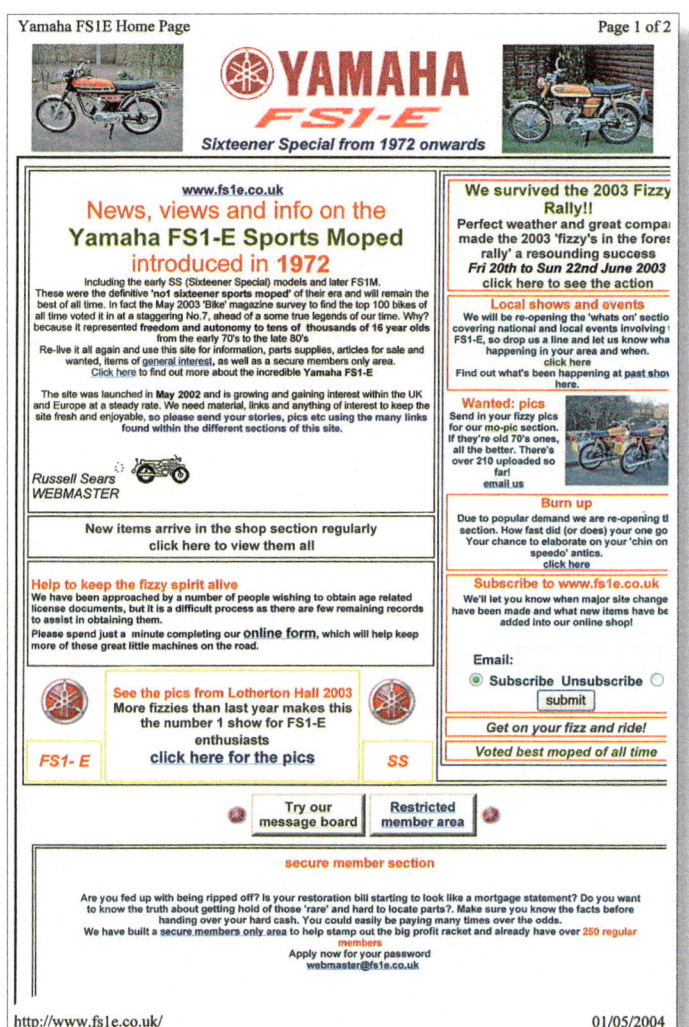

The Yamaha FS1-E website. The focal point of the FS1-E revival movement.

of the bits, and the time they take, but a restored fizzy costs a lot more than, say, a restored Suzuki GT750 watercooled, and it seems wrong somehow. Perhaps it's because the fizzy was only designed to last a year or so."

What is it about the FS1-E that makes it so popular more than 35 years after its creation in 1972? "The FS1-E was a special little bike." said Russell, "It harps back to the fact we were growing up. We rode pushbikes, then suddenly this thing arrived that turned you into someone to be reckoned with. It's only pieces of metal, but it carries a great deal of sentimentality. It's something I'll always have a great deal of affection for."

CHAPTER SEVEN
SLOPEDS

"The bikes had got too fast, and the Government had to do something, so they changed the law to bring the speed down and said forget the pedal bit." - Terry Silvester.

"The net came down in 1977 and a few slipped under it. The sports moped era lasted another year, or two, on second-hand bikes, and when they were wrecked it dropped right off. The 'slopeds' weren't popular. You could go almost as fast on a racing push-bike." - Brent Fielder.

As well as having a capacity of less than 50cc, any moped registered after 1 August 1977 had to carry a plate declaring it to be a moped, effectively warranting that its 'maximum speed, in still air and on level ground carrying a rider weighing 75kg, does not exceed 30mph by more than 5mph'.

After the revised legislation came into effect, mopeds for 16-year-olds continued to look sporty even if they went slowly. There were some completely new models, but, to begin with

Puch's Monza was a modified Grand Prix.

at least, most manufacturers adapted their current machines to comply with the new learner law, and brought out redesigns with changed or performance-restricting parts.

There were a number of ideas how best to do this. Lucas investigated a system which would allow good acceleration whilst restricting top end speed, but it was not developed commercially. Morini explored the possibility of using an electronic governor which restricted fuel flow at a preset road speed, but dropped the idea because it could be bypassed too easily, or removed altogether. In the end the methods of limiting the speed of sports mopeds to comply with the new legislation were pretty crude, usually consisting of smaller carburettors and inlets, and changes to porting and exhaust systems.

Beta brought out the MX4 moped in 1978. It was a good looking trail bike, but its tiny 12-tooth gearbox sprocket made it impossible for the machine to exceed 30mph, and necessitated a frantic flurry of gear changes to make any

Post legislation Gileras were fitted with Euro model footpeg assemblies, and looked pretty much the same as pre-restriction bikes.

Slopeds

First and last. Garelli's KL50 with a MkI Rekord. In unrestricted form, the KL50 was a potent and exciting little motorcycle. Anticipating the new legislation, this 'new generation' Garelli was not supplied to the UK during the sports moped era, despite having been available on the continent for some years.

progress at all. The same year *Motorcycle Mechanics* magazine reviewed a £27 go-faster kit for restricted Fantic Caballeros. The kit consisted of a larger carburettor, and a new air filter connection and throttle cable. Combined with chopping off a section of exhaust pipe, throttle response and breathing was dramatically improved, and an extra 18.5mph was obtained. Before the modifications, the £399 machine was out-dragged from traffic lights by a cyclist.

Given it was a fairly straightforward matter to derestrict most slopeds, how many riders did so?

"There wasn't much tuning or modifying done. People were terrified their insurance would be invalid, and parents wouldn't allow it. Apart from anything else most teenagers didn't have the technical know how - they were clueless." - Brent Fielder.

Terry Silvester disagrees. *"Kids would buy illegal big bore kits and change the exhausts. You wouldn't believe how many kids come in, even now, and ask for their learner bikes to be derestricted."*

"Kids soon wised up. They often had an older brother who told them what to do or they worked it out for themselves. Usually it was just a case of swapping to an earlier, or aftermarket, pipe or changing the front sprocket. They certainly didn't all crawl everywhere at 30mph." - Russell Marsden.

The DT50, Yamaha's post legislation trail moped, cost £340, in August 1978. It was a competent off-roader, handling

Funky Mopeds

Yamaha RD50 and DT50 slopeds.

Slopeds

mud, sand, bumps, potholes, and puddles with aplomb, and on the road the bike was capable of brisk acceleration, but its maximum indicated speed was a paltry 33mph on the flat - just what the government intended.

The road oriented RD50, which retailed for £370, achieved a maximum speedo reading of 34mph. With fast footwork, it could keep up with traffic from the lights, but it wouldn't rev beyond 7500rpm in top despite a 10,000 rev counter red line. Both bikes were well specified, and featured Yamaha's Autolube oil lubrication system.

As motorcycles improve and develop in general, so the advancements are incorporated into the designs of post legislation mopeds. Many are excellent little motorcycles. Some even have an X factor, that certain something that makes them stand out as special machines. They all have one thing in common, however, which ensures no-one will ever get excited about owning and riding them; they are gutless wonders, incapable of pulling the skin off a rice pudding.

It is for that reason, and that reason alone, that they cannot be called sports mopeds, which is why within a very few years, more or less by the end of the 1970s, the whole sports moped era came to an end ...

Honda replaced the SS50 with the CB50J.

Suzuki's GT50P took over from the AP50.

Gilera 50TS.

www.veloce.co.uk
Details of all Veloce books • New book news • Special offers • Newsletter

CHAPTER EIGHT
1970s SPORTS MOPEDS

AJW

AJW are the initials of founder Arthur John Wheaton, of Exeter, who formed his motorcycle business in 1926, as an offshoot of his family printing and publishing company.

In the 1970s, AJW operated from Wimborne, in Dorset. The south west concern claimed to be the first to bring Minarelli engines into the UK, and marketed a pair of exotic Italian sports mopeds made by Peripoli Brothers in Vicenza, Italy, but carrying the AJW name.

AJW Greyhound.

AJW Wolfhound.

The cafe racer style Greyhound had a race developed tubular chassis, and was very similar to the Guillietta Greyhound and the Testi Champion. It used the same cast iron barrel P6 Minarelli six speed engine as the Champion and the Fantic TI, but in a version specially manufactured for AJW with its own porting and exhaust pipe, designed for a top speed of over 50mph, and fuel consumption of 140mpg.

Available with tank and twin tool boxes in crimson Italian racing red, yellow or orange/bronze, with a black frame, the Greyhound was fitted with polished stainless steel mudguards, a choice of flat handlebars or clip-ons, and an adjustable seat. Unlike most Italian sports mopeds, it had a stop light.

The well-equipped AJW Wolfhound street scrambler featured adjustable rear suspension, long travel forks, and heavy duty rims and hubs, and came with a choice of trials, or motocross Pirelli tyres. Fitted with stone guards, a sump

1970s sports mopeds

protector and racing plates, the bike also boasted a competition speedo, cable adjusters in pouches on the control levers, and a tool bag and map case.

The Wolfhound was supplied in yellow or racing red with a silver frame, black leatherette side panels, and matt black handlebars, exhaust system, and swinging arm. An 80cc motorcycle version was also available.

The AJW Pointer de Luxe and Airedale were traditional mopeds, and the firm also marketed an unusual delivery moped called the Collie, which had two strong racks as standard fittings, and the 2.4bhp Whippet, which was similar to the Greyhound, but more suitable for commuting.

AJW GREYHOUND

Engine	Modified Minarelli P6 two-stroke
Bore and stroke	38.8 x 42mm
Power	6bhp@9000rpm
Carburettor	19mm Dell 'Orto
Gears	Six
Electrical system	6v 32 watt magneto/generator
Fuel capacity	10 litres
Weight	130lbs
Tyres	17 x 2.5 front, 17 x 2.75 rear
Max speed	55mph
Price	£269.00 in February 1977
Extras available	Longer seat, nose fairing, tuned barrel, and 20mm carburettor.

AJW WOLFHOUND

Engine	Modified Minarelli P6 two-stroke
Bore and stroke	38.8 x 42mm
Power	6bhp@9000rpm
Carburettor	19mm Dell 'Orto
Gears	Six
Electrical system	6v 32 watt magneto/generator
Fuel capacity	10 litres
Weight	140lbs
Tyres	2.5 or 2.75 x 19 front, 3 x 17 rear
Max speed	50mph
Price	£319.00 in February 1977
Extras available	Tuned barrel and 20mm carburettor, heavy duty motocross forks

BATAVUS

Batavus, the Dutch bicycle and moped manufacturer, can trace its origins back to 1904, when Andries Gaastra opened a shop in Heerenveen selling clocks, watches, and sewing machines. Gaastra later switched his attention to selling the German Presto bicycle, and later, bikes under his own brand name, Batavus. By World War Two, the firm had 120 employees.

Batavus Mk 4S.

Powered two-wheelers followed after the war.

Harglo Ltd, a UK importer set up in 1973 by two former BSA/Triumph executives, Wilf Harrison and Peter Glover, drew up the specification for the Batavus HS50. Essentially a step-through machine with a petrol tank in the conventional motorcycle position, it was fitted with a Dutch 48cc Laura M48-2 reed valve engine with cast iron barrel, and aluminium alloy head, which produced 2.4bhp. The bike had a single speed transmission with an automatic clutch, and could achieve 35mph.

Batavus's range topping Mk4S was a competent, and well-equipped, mini motorcycle with a spine frame, and oil damped suspension front and rear. Powered by a four speed Sachs engine fed by a Bing carburettor, its large petrol tank gave it a range of around 240 miles on two gallons of petrol. The bike had an electronic tachometer and indicators as standard equipment, an ignition switch and pedals, which both acted as kickstarters, and swung freely when used as

Funky Mopeds

Batavus HS50.

footrests, an arrangement that sometimes made reaching the foot controls a problem.

Harglo also imported the oddball, Batavus Bronco, an automatic chopper style bike with high rise bars and high back seat, which retailed for £149.90 in November 1974 and £182.00 in July 1977.

BATAVUS MK 4S

Engine	Sachs DFX two-stroke
Bore and stroke	38 x 42mm
Power	3bhp@6000rpm
Carburettor	Bing 18mm
Gears	Four
Electrical system	6v 23w flywheel magneto
Fuel capacity	2.4 gallons
Weight	160lb
Wheelbase	46 inches
Tyres	2.5 x 17 front, 2.75 x 17 rear
Max speed	46mph
Fuel consumption	100mpg
Price	£275.00 in November 1974, £335.00 in July 1977
Imported	August 1974 until July 1977

BATAVUS HS50

Engine	Laura M48-2 two-stroke
Power	2.4bhp@5000rpm
Carburettor	Encarwi S22
Gears	Single-speed automatic clutch
Electrical system	6v Bosch magneto/generator
Fuel capacity	5 litres
Weight	90lb/40kg
Tyres	20 x 2 front and rear

CASAL

Metalurgia Casal was formed in 1953, in Aviero in Portugal, to produce engines for agricultural and industrial use. The first Casal vehicle was a two-stroke scooter produced in 1964, and

Casal S2.

Casal SS4.

1970s sports mopeds

Casal Phantom 5.

Casal ST50.

the firm manufactured its first moped in 1967. The company used its own engines and cycle components in its mopeds and motorcycles, but similarities between its engines and Zundapp units are not coincidental, the German company having supplied advisers and technicians to the Portuguese factory over many years.

Casal sports mopeds were among the first available in the UK, but never sold in large numbers. In January 1975, the early spine frame K190 four speed and K196 two speed models were revamped and relaunched as the SS4 and S2 respectively, and the purposeful motocross style ST50 was introduced. Featuring twin leading shoe brakes and alloy rims, the high specification 6.5bhp Phantom 5 joined the range five months later.

The SS4 was solid, reliable, and an impressive performer, capable of a top speed of around 48mph. Handling was good on smooth surfaces, but lively on bumps due to the bike's light steering and stiff suspension. Finish was good. Electrics and lighting were bad!

CASAL S2
Engine	49.9cc two-stroke
Power	2.5bhp
Gears	Two (hand change)
Tyres	2.75 x 17 front and rear

CASAL SS4
Engine	49.9cc two-stroke
Bore and stroke	40 x 39.7
	Light alloy head and barrel with chrome bore
Power	5.3bhp@7500rpm
Carburettor	17mm with plunger choke
Electrical system	Flywheel magneto ignition. 30w generator direct lighting
Gears	Four
Tyres	2.75 x 17 front and rear
Price	£215.00 in March 1975, £249.00 in July 1977
Imported	From January 1975 onwards

CASAL PHANTOM 5
Engine	49.9cc two-stroke
Power	6.2bhp@7500rpm
Gears	Five
Brakes	Twin shoe front and rear
Tyres	300 x 17 (alloy rims)
Max speed	55mph
Price	£299.00 in July 1977
Imported	From June 1975 onwards

CASAL ST50 CROSS
Engine	49.9cc two-stroke
Power	5.3bhp@7500rpm
Gears	Four
Tyres	3 x 17 front and rear
Max speed	35mph
Fuel consumption	120mpg
Price	£149.90 in November 1974

CIMATTI
Cimatti, an Italian family business founded in 1937 by

Funky Mopeds

Cimatti Kaiman and Sagittario.

successful bicycle racer Marco Cimatti to build pushbikes, constructed its first motorcycles in 1950.

The company's Minarelli powered Kaiman and Sagittario sports mopeds were imported from mid-1975 onwards. Well finished, and featuring neatly made duplex frames, they were tough, high quality machines.

The rugged 6bhp Kaiman trail bike offered 50mph road performance, and was also a useful off-road tool. It had a short wheelbase of only 48.5 inches, but was controllable and fun to ride up to around 30mph on the dirt, even over bumpy or rutted ground. This was thanks to excellent and progressive suspension front and rear. The bike sported Marzocchi forks and adjustable Sebac rear shock absorbers, and had practical fold back footpegs, and a rubber mounted rear light, but the low resting place of the non-locking left starting pedal was an off-road hazard.

CIMATTI KAIMAN

Engine	Minarelli P6
Power	6bhp@8500rpm
Carburettor	19mm Dell'Orto
Gears	Six
Electrical system	6v flywheel magneto
Fuel capacity	1.5 gallons
Weight	171lbs
Wheelbase	48.5 inches
Tyres	2.5 x 19 front, 3 x 17 rear
Max speed	50mph
Price	£295.92 in July 1977
Imported	From June 1975 until July 1977

CIMATTI SAGITTARIO

Engine	Minarelli P6
Power	6bhp
Carburettor	19mm Dell'Orto
Gears	Six
Electrical system	6v flywheel magneto
Fuel capacity	2 gallons
Weight	137lbs
Tyres	2.5 x 18 front and rear

1970s sports mopeds

Derbi Cross.

Max speed	50-55mph
Price	£253.80 in July 1976, £259 in July 1977
Imported	From June 1975 to July 1977

Available with high bars or clip-ons

CIMATTI BOBCAT

Engine	Morini
Gears	Four
Imported	From June 1975 to July 1977

DERBI

The Spanish Derbi concern imported its GT4 and Cross sports mopeds in small numbers.

DERBI GT4

Racy sports moped, and one of the cheapest 'sixteener specials.'

Power	4.5bhp
Speed	47mph
Price	£243 in July 1977
Imported	April 1975 to February 1977

DERBI CROSS

Racy sports moped, and one of the cheapest 'sixteener specials.'

Power	4.5bhp
Speed	47mph
Price	£286 in July 1977
Imported	February 1976 to February 1977

FANTIC MOTOR

Fantic Motor was created by Henry Keppel and Mario Agrati in 1968, in a new plant in Barzago near Milan, in northern Italy. The pair began by manufacturing fun bikes aimed at the USA market, and produced a successful range of mini bikes, including trikes and choppers, before building their first real motorcycles in 1971.

The first bikes were 50cc and 100cc Caballeros, and the Diablo-Cross, and Ranger. In November the same year, the Chopper and TI (Turismo Internazionale) were launched at the Milan Motorcycle Show. Both new models were 50cc high compression two stroke singles with four-speed gearboxes. The TI put out 5bhp@7500rpm, and the Chopper was tuned to produce 6.8bhp@8800rpm. A 125cc version of the Chopper was introduced in 1973.

In 1975, two new 50cc Caballeros were brought onto the market; the 7.2bhp Regolarita Competizione, which had Marzocchi suspension, electronic ignition, and a new motor (TX160) that produced 9bhp@10,200rpm, and a detuned version. The GT Super Six began production in mid-1976. The bike had a six speed engine that produced 9.14bhp@9500rpm, and was capable of 95kph. It sported alloy wheels and a disc front brake. The following year the Super Six was available in 9.5 and 7.2bhp forms. By 1977, the company had a 14 bike range, of which only two were minibikes, and the now enlarged factory was producing 200 machines a day, and employed around 200 people.

The six speed Minarelli engined TI and Chopper sports mopeds, which were first imported to the UK in December 1972, were fast, but temperamental. Their iron barrels didn't dissipate heat efficiently enough, and their piston rings would break up if they were thrashed for any length of time. Aluminium barrels on later models solved the problem.

The Turismo Internazionale was well finished, and was supplied with a silver duplex frame, and a choice of vivid orange, yellow, green, or purple paintwork. Large angular fins gave the engine an appearance of greater size, and it was altogether an attractive bike with a proper motorcycle feel. The engine gave a broad spread of power, but close gear ratios meant flurries of gear changes were needed to keep the bike moving. The reward was a top speed of between 50

Funky Mopeds

and 55mph on the flat, and more than 60mph was achievable downhill. Early bikes had six speed gearboxes, but this option was discontinued in late 1974, and the four speed gearbox version, which had been introduced in March 1974, continued to be imported until February 1977. Both boxes shared the same first, second, and top gears.

Handling was adequate though bouncy on bumpy roads, and the TI's brakes were reasonably efficient, but the bike had a generally poor electrical system, terrible lights, a tiny and over optimistic Veglia speedometer, and a useless horn. A carb mounted choke lever was pushed down to click on and automatically snapped off when the throttle was fully opened. The pedals, which were used to start the bike, swung back and forth, making it difficult to reach the gear lever or brake pedal. Theoretically, they could also be used to pedal the machine, but in reality, it was difficult to get enough momentum to stay upright.

Imported from January 1974 to February 1977, the Fantic Super T was a sportier and more powerful variation of the TI, with an upswept expansion chamber exhaust. It was only available with a four speed gearbox and was rare then, and even rarer today.

With its powerful Minarelli engine pulling strongly as it screamed through its six gears, the Fantic Chopper was a fast moped, managing around 50mph despite its shape and bulk. It was also incredibly loud. Surprisingly, it handled well, and, although it had a 57 inch wheelbase, it was easily manoeuvrable. Braking performance was adequate, though different braking rules applied, with the rear having to work harder than normal because of the design of the bike, and the front was spongy due to its long cable. Once the technique was mastered, the bike could be hauled up efficiently without skidding the five inch rear tyre. The engine pulled from as little as 1500rpm, but real power came in at 6000rpm, and ran out at its 9000rpm maximum. Fuel economy was good; just as well considering the small tank, and the bike returned around 120mpg no matter how much it was thrashed. Like the TI, the electrics were poor, with no stoplight, but the overall finish of the Chopper was good.

First imported in August 1974, the Caballero 50 was one of the first enduro mopeds, and probably the best. It was a competent off-road machine, and faster than just about all other sports mopeds on the road, only being caught by more street-biased bikes on the twistiest of roads. It was noisy with a distinctive hammering sound, but was comfortable, smooth, and stable, and gave the impression of being a much larger machine.

The Caballero's pedals were easy to use to start the bike's Minarelli engine, but were free swinging when used as footpegs, and led to the occasional fluffed gear change. Otherwise both four and six speed close ratio gearboxes the bike was supplied with were sweet to use, and, together with the engine's trademark broad spread of power, allowed brisk acceleration to a top speed of around 55mph.

Although Caballeros were excellent bikes, they had a generally poor electrical system and switchgear, and blew bulbs regularly. They were also expensive.

Available only to special order, the Super Caballero 50 was a 9bhp version that cost £475.00 in July 1977. It was fitted with a kickstart, and had no pedals, so did not qualify as a moped. The higher specification Caballero 50 RC (TX160) enduro racer produced 12bhp at 10,000rpm, and cost £549.00.

The Fantic GT (Gran Turismo TX201) was long established in Italy, before being exported to the UK from summer 1975. Described by *Motorcycle Mechanics* in April 1977 as the closest a moped will ever get to a real motorcycle, the GT was faster than the TI and other Fantic models that preceded it, but a lot more smooth and comfortable. It had a big bike feel, and was, for a Fantic, relatively quiet. It was reliable and easy to start, and, once on the move, the controls were positive and responsive.

With alloy wheels, front disc brake, rev counter, and electronic ignition, the fantastic Fantic GT Super Six was a high specification version of the standard Fantic GT, and also considerably more powerful than the model it was derived from. The Super Six's 38.8mm x 42mm 9bhp Minarelli engine produced usable power of between 6000rpm and 12,000rpm, peaking at around 10,000rpm.

The bike was capable of 65-70mph, and handled well, but sold in only small numbers in Great Britain due to its high price, and late arrival on the sports moped scene. The bike had been sold in Italy for some time, but wasn't introduced to the UK market until six months before the new learner rules came into force in August 1977. It is understood Fantic, and its UK importer, held the model back to avoid antagonising the British Government while the new legislation was being drafted, but when the revised regulations were announced, the company decided to sell the Super Six in Britain in the time it had left.

FANTIC TI

Engine	Minarelli
Power	6bhp@9000rpm
Carburettor	14mm Dell'Orto
Gears	Six/four
Electrical system	6v 18w flywheel magneto
Fuel capacity	1.1 gallons
Weight	139lb
Wheelbase	46 inches
Tyres	2.75 x 17 front and rear

Fantic TI.

Fantic Chopper.

Fantic Super T.

Funky Mopeds

Fantic Caballero.

Fantic GT.

Fantic GT Super Six (inset: note condom pocket in the seat!).

1970s sports mopeds

Max speed	55mph
Price	£209.95 in June 1974
Imported	
6 speed	December 1972 to October 1974
4 speed	March 1974 to February 1977

A kit consisting of a 19mm Dell 'Orto carburettor, and an alternative inlet manifold and air filter would boost the power to 7.2bhp and give better acceleration, together with enhanced induction roar and engine howl.

FANTIC SUPER T

Engine	Minarelli
Power	7.2bhp@9000rpm
Carburettor	19mm Dell 'Orto
Gears	Four
Electrical system	6v 18w flywheel magneto
Fuel capacity	1.1 gallons
Weight	139lbs
Wheelbase	46 inches
Tyres	2.75 x 17 front and rear
Max speed	60mph
Price	£246.00 in January 1976
Imported	January 1974 to February 1977

FANTIC CHOPPER

Engine	Minarelli
Power	6.8bhp@8,800rpm
Carburettor	19mm Dell 'Orto
Gears	Six
Electrical system	6v 18w flywheel magneto
Fuel capacity	1.1 gallons
Weight	80kg
Wheelbase	1425mm (static)
Tyres	2.75 x 16 front, 5 x 16 rear
Max speed	52mph
Fuel consumption	125mpg
Price	£279.95 in December 1972
Imported	December 1972 to October 1974

FANTIC CABALLERO 50

Engine	Minarelli two-stroke
Power	7.2bhp
Carburettor	19mm Dell 'Orto
Electrical system	Flywheel magneto
Gears	Four/six
Fuel capacity	1.7 gallons
Weight	168lbs
Wheelbase	49.5 inches
Tyres	2.5 x 19 front, 3 x 17 rear
Max speed	55mph
Price	£329.00 July 1976
Imported	From August 1974

FANTIC GT

Engine	Minarelli two-stroke
Power	7.2bhp@8000rpm
Carburettor	Dell 'Orto
Gears	Four
Fuel capacity	1.7 gallons
Weight	147lbs (dry)
Wheelbase	49 inches
Max speed	60.5mph
Price	£325.00 in April 1977, £334.00 in July 1977
Imported	From July 1975 to February 1977

FANTIC GT SUPER SIX

Engine	Minarelli two-stroke
Power	9bhp@10,000rpm
Bore and stroke	38.8 x 42mm
Compression ratio	13:1
Carburettor	Dell 'Orto
Gears	Six
Fuel capacity	1.7 gallons
Weight	182lbs
Max speed	65mph
Price	£579.00
Imported	February 1977 to February 1979

FLANDRIA

Flandria is the Latin word for Flanders, the northern Dutch speaking part of Belgium, and also the name of a small motorcycle manufacturing company founded there, in the 1950s, by Aime and Remi Claeys. Using their own engine, they manufactured a 49cc two-seater moped with a hand operated clutch. Later, the brothers fell out and became competitors. Aime kept the Claeys engine, and Remi created Superia, a new brand that used Sachs engines.

A. Claeys-Flandria became the leading motorcycle manufacturer in the Benelux countries with factories at Zedelgen and Zwevezele, near Bruges, producing 110,000 motorcycles and mopeds a year, as well as bicycles, lawnmowers, and gas heaters. There were also plants in France, Morocco, Portugal, and Holland. The powerful engine was also constructed under licence at Figuaras, in Spain. The company went bankrupt in 1981.

A number of Flandria sports moped models were imported into the UK, and sold through various outlets including home shopping catalogues.

Funky Mopeds

Flandria 547M.

Flandria 547L.

FLANDRIA 547M
Engine	A. Claeys two-stroke
Power	3.6bhp@7,200
Gears	Four
Fuel capacity	1.5 gallons
Weight	128lbs
Wheelbase	45.7 inches
Tyres	2.25 x 17 front, 2.5 x 17 rear
Max speed	45mph
Price	Not known

FLANDRIA 547L
Engine	A. Claeys two-stroke
Power	3.6bhp@7200
Gears	Four
Fuel capacity	1.5 gallons
Weight	141lbs
Wheelbase	45.7 inches
Tyres	2.25 x 17 front, 2.5 x 17 rear
Max speed	45mph
Price	Not known

Importation dates for Flandria models
Scorpion M	March 1974 to August 1975
SP547M	July 1974 to April 1976
SP547LM	March 1974 to April 1976
SP547LMS	September 1974 to April 1976

GARELLI

In 1912, Italian engineer Adalberto Garelli designed his own two-stroke engine, and patented a gear change system, before building prototype motorcycles between 1914-18, and founding a factory to manufacture his designs in Milan in 1919. Garelli motorcycles achieved national and international success in the 1920s ridden by, among others, the great racing driver, Tazio Nuvolari. In 1962, Garelli merged with Agrati,

Garelli Rekord Mk I.

1970s sports mopeds

Garelli Rekord Mk II.

the largest bicycle parts manufacturer in Italy, and went on to produce a comprehensive range of mopeds and lightweight motorcycles.

Garelli sports mopeds were imported into Britain by Agrati Sales (UK) Ltd, and the first were the Rekord and Tiger Cross. The Garelli Rekord Mk I had been sold in Britain since April 1969, in motorcycle form with a kickstart and footpegs, and Agrati added pedals in 1972 to convert the model into a UK specification moped. It was one of the first sports mopeds in the UK, and one of the fastest, capable of around 60mph on the flat. The bike was given a makeover, and continued in Mk II form from late 1973.

The distinctive yellow and black Garelli Tiger Cross arrived in the UK in June 1972, and was an instant success. If the Yamaha FS1-E tops the podium as the archetypal 1970s sports moped, the Tiger Cross is the runner-up. It was a budget bike, as was clear from its castings, machinings, and general build quality, but it had plenty of horsepower, and was as quick and capable as the Rekord. It was modern, stylish and purposeful looking with its bright colour scheme, knobbly tyres and motocross looks. Sixteeners loved it.

From September 1975 onwards, the Garelli Rekord Cross joined the range. As its name implies, it was a combination of the established Rekord and Tiger Cross. The Tiger Special, which was essentially a Tiger Cross facelift model, went on the market in January 1976. In early 1977, the extremely rapid five speed Garelli KL50 trail moped had long been on sale in Italy when it was introduced to the UK. From August 1977, it was sold in restricted form to comply with the changed learner legislation.

GARELLI REKORD MK I

Garelli Tiger Cross Mk I.

Funky Mopeds

Garelli Tiger Cross Mk II.

Garelli Tiger Special.

1970s sports mopeds

Garelli Rekord Cross.

1969 to late 1973
- Top speed   60mph (fractionally faster than the Tiger Cross due to gearing and wheel size).
- Tyres   2.25 x 19 front, 2.5 x 19 rear
- (80cc version available)

GARELLI REKORD MK II
From late 1973 onwards.
- Differences from MkI
  - Seat
  - Chainguard
  - Grips
  - Side panels
  - Tank
  - Price   £246.00 in July 1977

GARELLI TIGER CROSS MK I
First imported in June 1972
- Power   6.5bhp
- Lower section of tank painted gloss black
- Polished aluminium engine casings
- Melon grips
- First 900 out of factory had hydraulic damped Ceriani forks (later ones had 'pogo sticks')
- First 400 had leather sprung seats
- (Also 800 MK1.5 versions with in-between forks)

GARELLI TIGER CROSS MK II

Funky Mopeds

Power 6.5bhp
Differences from Mk I
  Black decal strip along bottom of tank containing name
  Black engine casings
  Thinner grips
  Slightly altered seat
  Slightly altered rear shock absorbers
  Pogo forks - more modern looking, but just springs and tubes, and handled less well
Price £246.00 in July 1977

From 1975 onwards the Tiger Cross became available in different colours, and the mudguards were painted instead of stainless steel.

GARELLI TIGER SPECIAL

January 1976 onwards
Power 6.5bhp
UK only facelift model
  Painted high rise mudguard
  Extra bolt on exhaust
  Different exhaust guard and baffle
  Deep finned barrel
  Special Dellorto carburettor
  Available in matt black, red or trendy green

GARELLI REKORD CROSS

September 1975 onwards

GILERA

In 1909, near Monza in Italy, the historic Gilera marque was founded by Count Guiseppe Gilera. In the 1950s, Gilera machines won multiple 500cc world championships, and had TT wins in the hands of Geoff Duke and Bob MacIntyre. In 1970, Gilera was taken over by Piaggio, the maker of mopeds and Vespa scooters, and the firm then concentrated on mopeds and lightweight motorcycles.

Gilera Touring and Trials sports mopeds were imported to the UK from mid-1972, and the Enduro model was added to the British range two years later. They were well built, and had an air of quality, but delivered rather tame performance because the company restricted its dependable and tractable 50cc engines to 4.2bhp@5500rpm for the British moped market by using tiny inlet and transfer ports. Motorcycle versions with footpegs produced 6.2bhp@7500rpm.

The Gileras's neat twin cradle frames were sturdy and well made, and the engines, which had alloy barrels and heads, were robust, easy to start, and reliable. The pedals locked into position as footrests, the brakes were adequate, and all early bikes had Ceriani front and rear suspension, and

Gilera sold three moped versions of the sturdy 50cc motorcycle.

good quality Tomassi control levers. The general attention to detail and standard of finish was first class. Negative points included push-bike style speedometers, a pathetic horn that dimmed the lights, and lack of mirrors, indicators, and an ignition switch. The chain adjustment system also came in for criticism; it was flimsy, and its cam tended to loosen. Economy versions were imported from June 1976, which used non-adjustable levers, and cheap, pressed steel grease damped forks instead of the oil damped Ceriani forks fitted on the full price models.

The Trial and Enduro drew praise from testers as good green laning machines, and all three models were agile and manoeuvrable, extremely user-friendly, and excellent learner bikes.

GILERA RS50 TOURING MOPED

Engine   49.79cc two-stroke
Power   4.2bhp@5500rpm
Bore and stroke   38.4mm x 43mm
Carburettor   Dell'Orto SHB18
Gears   Four
Electrical system   6v 25w flywheel magneto
Fuel capacity   1.5 gallons
Weight   68kg
Wheelbase   1160mm max
Max speed   42mph
Price   £209.95 in June 1974
                    £264.00 in July 1977

1970s sports mopeds

Gilera Touring. Gilera Enduro. Gilera Trial.

Economy version   £242.00 April 1977
                  £250.00 July 1977)

Price   £283.50 in July 1976
                  £291.00 in July 1977

GILERA RS50 TRIAL MOPED
Engine	49.79cc two-stroke
Power	4.2bhp@5500rpm
Bore and stroke	38.4mm x 43mm
Carburettor	Dell 'Orto SHB18
Gears	Four
Electrical system	6v 25w flywheel magneto
Fuel capacity	1.5 gallons
Weight	68kg
Wheelbase	46.5 inches
Tyres	2.5 x 19 front, 3 x 17 rear
Max speed	42mph
Fuel consumption	96mpg
Price	£215.00 in July 1974
	£285.00 in July 1977
Economy version	£264.00

GILERA RS50 ENDURO MOPED
Engine	49.79cc two-stroke
Power	4.2bhp@6000rpm
Bore and stroke	38.4mm x 43mm
Carburettor	Dell 'Orto SHB18
Gears	Four
Electrical system	6v 25w flywheel magneto
Fuel capacity	1.5 gallons
Weight	176lbs
Wheelbase	47.5 inches
Tyres	2.5 x 19 front, 3 x 17 rear
Max speed	45mph

GITANE

Gitanes were basically Testis, assembled in France under licence. Apart from different paintwork, graphics, and small mechanical modifications, they were essentially the same bikes. Later Gitane was bought by Renault, and the French-built machines were marketed as the Gitane Elf.

At around £100 more than a Yamaha FS1-E, the faired and streamlined Gitane Champion Veloce was an expensive bike, and a rare sight on British roads. With its rev counter, six speed gearbox, alloy wheels, disc brakes, and cantilever monoshock suspension, it was advanced for its time, and probably the ultimate cafe racer sports moped. Like a lot of Italian mopeds, it used a 6.2bhp Minarelli P6 engine, but its ultra light weight and high gearing made it faster at top speed than the competition, allegedly managing almost 70mph. Lights were poor.

The Champion, Trail King, and Grand Sport completed the sports moped range.

GITANE CHAMPION VELOCE
Engine	Minarelli P6
Power	6.2bhp
Price	£369.00 in summer 1977

GITANE CHAMPION
Engine	Minarelli P6
Power	6.2bhp@8500rpm
Bore and stroke	38.8 x 42mm
Carburettor	Dell 'Orto SHB19-19D

Funky Mopeds

Badge engineering. Gitanes were basically French-built Testis.

Gitane Champion Veloce. (Courtesy Ian Ritchie)

Gitane Champion. (Courtesy Ian Ritchie)

1970s sports mopeds

Gitane Grand Sport.   **Gitane Trail King.**

Gears	Six
Electrical system	Flywheel magneto
Tyres	2.5 x 17 front, 2.5 x 17 rear
Price	£289.00 in July 1977
Imported	October 1975 to July 1977

GITANE TRAIL KING

Engine	Minarelli P6
Power	6.2bhp@8500rpm
Bore and stroke	8.8 x 42mm
Carburettor	Dell 'Orto SHB19-19D
Gears	Six
Electrical system	Flywheel magneto
Tyres	2.5 x 19 front, 2.5 x 17 rear
Price	£315.00 in July 1977
Imported	From October 1975 to July 1977

GITANE GRAND SPORT

Engine	Minarelli
Power	5.6bhp@9000rpm
Bore and stroke	38.8mm x 42mm
Carburettor	Dell 'Orto SHB19-19D
Gears	Four
Electrical system	Flywheel magneto
Tyres	2.5 x 17 front and rear
Price	£229.00 in July 1977
Imported	October 1975 to July 1977

HONDA

In 1946, Soichiro Honda sold his profitable war-time piston ring business, and bought 500 war surplus two-stroke engines, and adapted them for use on bicycles. He then designed his own two-stroke engine, and in 1948 established the Honda Motor Company Ltd, which went on to become the largest manufacturer of motorcycles in the world.

Honda took a responsible line regarding the performance of its sports moped, the SS50, and the model's sleek looks belied its feeble performance. As a result, sixteeners riding the only four-stroke machine on the market were condemned to being blown off by every other sports moped that came across them. So owning the 2.5bhp SS50 did not carry a great deal of street cred. A simple carburettor modification would increase available throttle movement and release more power, but most stayed in the slow lane.

The four speed Honda SS50 may have been pathetically slow, but not having to get involved with mixing oil and petrol on the forecourt was a definite plus point of four-stroke ownership. Also, the SS50 was quiet, economical, reliable, and easy to live with, apart from a kickstart that folded up in use, resulting in shins getting skinned on the right footpedal. Similar in appearance to the Yamaha FS1-E, it had a pressed steel frame, slimline petrol tank, and pedals that locked as footrests in an ideal position in relation to gear and brake pedals. A spring-loaded cam on the pedal crank was turned through 180 degrees, and secured by a locking pin and lever on the left side of the engine. The bike had ultra narrow 22

Honda SS50 4 speed.

Funky Mopeds

Honda SS50 ZB2. (Courtesy Matt Chambers)

inch handlebars.

The SS50 ZB2 was a faster upgrade model that produced 4bhp@9000rpm. It had a well spaced five speed gearbox, and would reach between 45 and 50mph and still return 138mpg. An efficient 9.5 inch cable operated front disc brake replaced the 110mm drum on the earlier bike, and wider rubber mounted bars were fitted that, together with spongy suspension, gave a peculiar, bouncy ride. The headlight and electrics in general were praiseworthy.

HONDA SS50

Engine	OHC 4-stroke
Power	2.5bhp@8000rpm
Bore and stroke	39 x 41.4mm
Carburettor	Keihin 12mm
Electrical system	6v AC generator
Gears	Four
Fuel capacity	1.5 gallons
Weight	176lbs
Wheelbase	45.5 inches
Tyres	2.5 x 17 front and rear
Max speed	39mph
Fuel consumption	144mpg
Price	£210.00 in March 1975

HONDA SS50 ZB2

Engine	OHC 4-stroke
Power	4bhp@9000rpm
Bore and stroke	39 x 41.4mm
Carburettor	Keihin 12mm
Electrical system	Flywheel magneto
Gears	Six
Fuel capacity	1.5 gallons
Weight	167lbs
Wheelbase	46.5 inches
Tyres	2.5 x 17 front and rear
Max speed	50mph
Fuel consumption	138mpg
Price	£259.00 in July 1976

KREIDLER

The West German Kreidler concern had a tremendous racing pedigree, and prided itself on high engineering standards. The moped and small motorcycle specialist put its design emphasis on reliability and long life, and ran an award scheme for owners completing 100,000 kilometres on their machines.

Alfred Kreidler began manufacturing mopeds in 1950, and later built a 50cc racing bike, winning the first ever 50cc Grand Prix in Barcelona in 1962, and almost taking the title again the following year. The 1964 model was a twin with 14 gears, which was capable of well over 100mph, but despite further successes the firm found itself unable to compete with the budgets of the Japanese factory teams, and withdrew from GPs in 1965. That year a supercharged and streamlined Kreidler set a 50cc speed record of 140.02mph on the Utah Salt Flats.

In 1969, new regulations restricting the maximum number of gears and cylinders came into effect in Grand Prix racing, and Kreidler re-entered the championship. Jan de Vries won the 50cc championship in 1971 and 1973, and Kreidler dominated the class from 1973 to 1975. Barry Sheene won the Czechoslovakian GP on a Kreidler in 1971. In 1974, at Spa Francorchamps, that year's world champion, Henk van

A redesign and an extra gear got Honda's SS50 on the pace.

1970s sports mopeds

Kreidler Florett. (Courtesy Alan Fleet)

riding, and the brakes were first class.

KREIDLER SUPER SPORTS DELUXE

Engine	Kreidler two-stroke
Power	4bhp@7500rpm
Carburettor	Bing 14mm
Electrical system	6v flywheel magneto, 24 watt generator
Gears	Four
Fuel capacity	2.75 gallons
Weight	180lbs (dry)
Wheelbase	47.5 inches
Tyres	2.75 x 17 front and rear
Max speed	48mph
Price	£244 .00 in August 1974
Imported	
RM Sports	Jan 1974 to Jan 1977
RM Tourer	Jan 1974 to Jan 1977
RM Cross	Jan 1975 to Jan 1977

KTM

KTM began producing motorcycles in Mattighofen, Austria in 1951, and has been successful in road racing and motocross competition. The company produced a comprehensive range of pedal powered machines, and was part of the scooter boom of the 1960s.

KTM used Sachs engines in its moped range.

Kessel, was timed at 125.5mph, and set a lap record speed of 101.07mph on his Van Veen Kreidler. His six speed watercooled, single cylinder, disc valve machine produced 21bhp at the crankshaft, and had a powerband from 14,000 to 17,000rpm. Kreidler also won the 50cc manufacturers' award from 1971 to 1976 inclusive.

Road-going Kreidlers remained popular in Germany until the 1980s, but the firm was increasingly unable to keep pace with the Japanese competition, and went out of business in 1983.

Like all Kreidlers, the UK specification four speed Super Sports Deluxe was a quality machine, well designed, soundly engineered, and finished to a high standard. It was easily capable of 45mph, but the European model, which had five gears, had a maximum speed of over 55mph. As well as having a strong race bred engine, the bike handled superbly. It had a pressed steel frame, sturdy telescopic forks with progressive damping, and rear shock absorbers that were strong enough to carry a passenger. The excellent lights enabled fast night

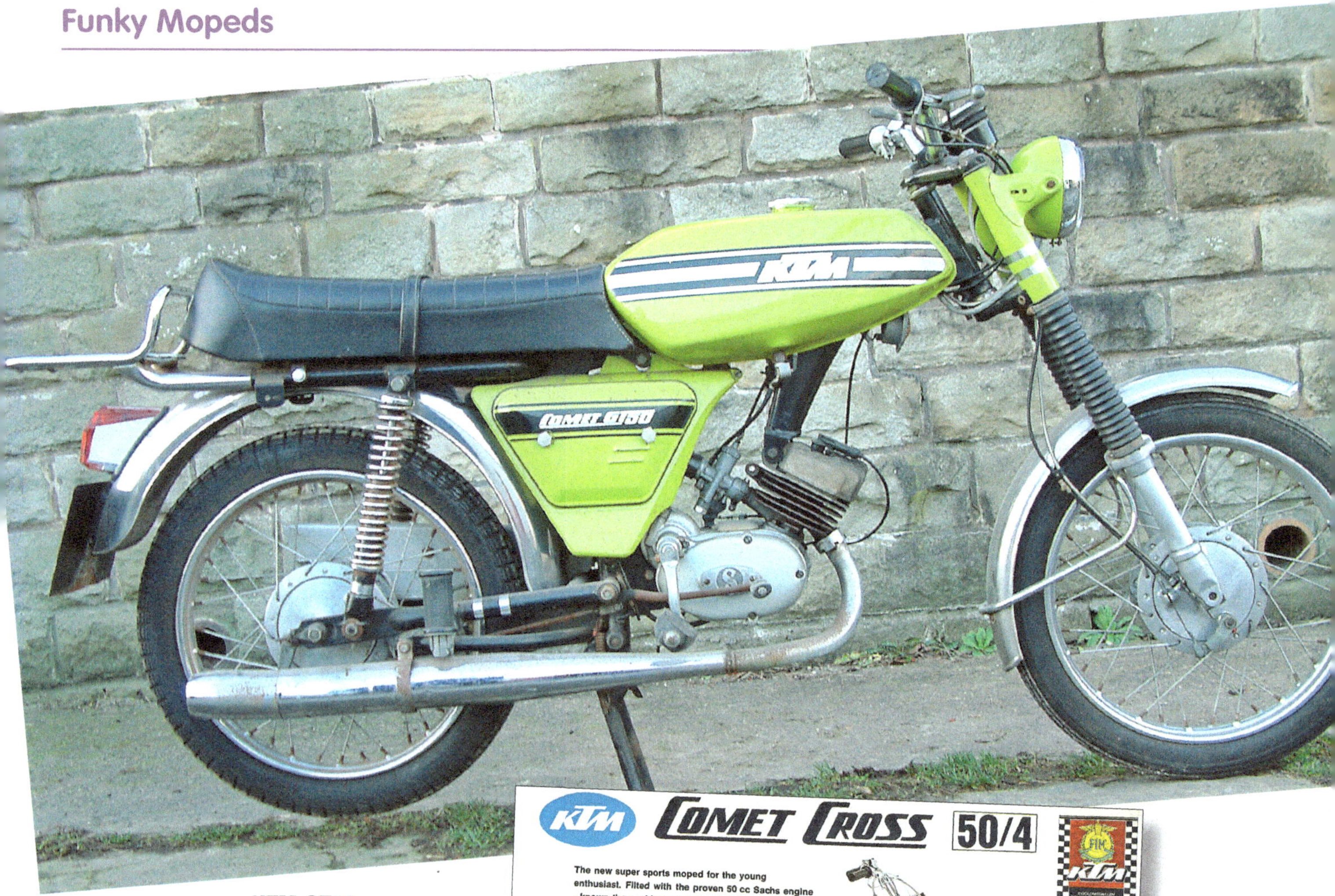
KTM
COMET GT50

KTM GT50.

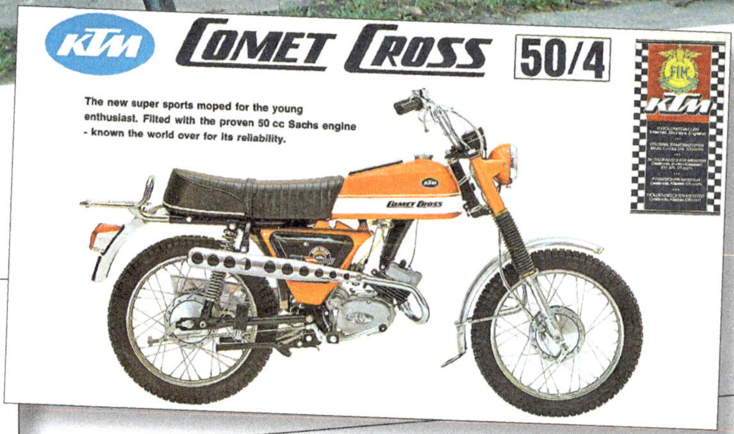
KTM
COMET CROSS
50/4
The new super sports moped for the young enthusiast. Fitted with the proven 50 cc Sachs engine - known the world over for its reliability.
KTM
Comet Cross

KTM Comet Cross.

KTM GT50 De Luxe.

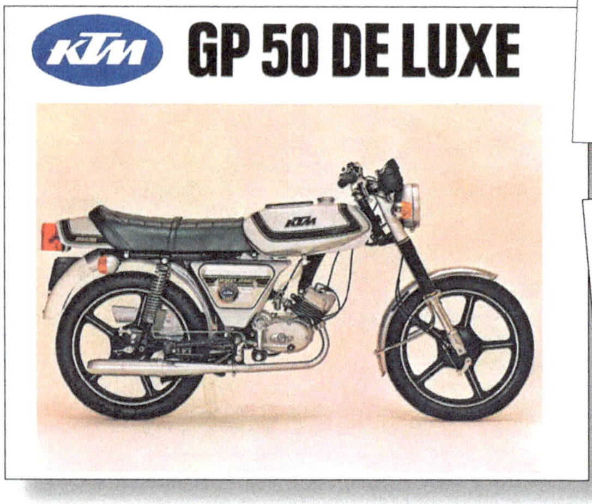
KTM
GP 50 DE LUXE
KTM

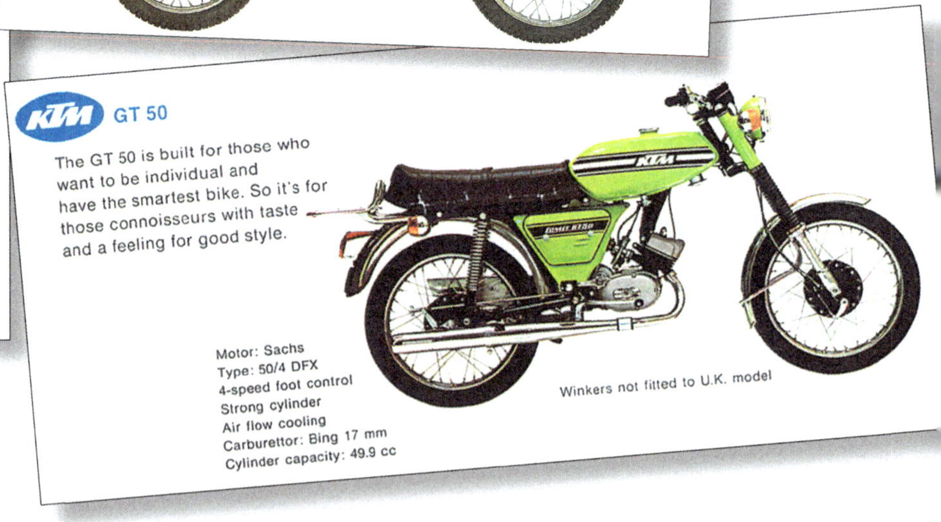
KTM
GT 50
The GT 50 is built for those who want to be individual and have the smartest bike. So it's for those connoisseurs with taste and a feeling for good style.
KTM
Motor: Sachs
Type: 50/4 DFX
4-speed foot control
Strong cylinder
Air flow cooling
Carburettor: Bing 17 mm
Cylinder capacity: 49.9 cc
Winkers not fitted to U.K. model

KTM GT50.

1970s sports mopeds

The Comet range of mopeds was launched in 1964. Styled as lightweight motorcycles, they were powered by 50cc two-stroke Sachs engines. A step-through range, called the Hobby, was put on the market in 1967.

In 1972, KTM developed its first home made engine, a 175cc two-stroke single, which was successful from the start in motocross. By the end of the sports moped era, the factory had won 20 national motocross titles, the 1976 International Six Day Trial, the 1976 Motocross Manufacturers' Championship, and the Russian, Gennady Moisseev, had been world 250cc motocross champion in 1974 and 1977.

KTM COMET CROSS
Imported May 1973 to October 1976

KTM COMET GT
Imported July 1973 to February 1974

KTM COMET GRAND PRIX
Imported May 1974 to October 1976

KTM COMET GRAND PRIX DE LUXE
Imported July 1975 to October 1976

MALAGUTI

Founded by Antonio Malaguti in Bolgna in 1932 as a bicycle manufacturer, Malaguti began producing motorcycles in 1937, and by the mid-1970s had become the third largest manufacturer of mopeds in Italy. Malaguti sports mopeds used engines made by the Franco Morini company of Casaleccio di Reno, and were first imported to the UK at the beginning of 1974.

The sporty Malaguti Olympique had a huge 2.5 gallon tank, and a distinctive twin silencer exhaust system, and was available in two versions. The TR was fitted with raised bars, and the GT featured clip-on handlebars which, together with a fairing as an optional extra, completed the bike's cafe racer look. The Olympique's Morini iron-barrelled engine was fitted with a large Dell 'Orto carburettor, and produced 6.5bhp@8500rpm. The bike could manage more than 50mph, but the engine was gutless at low revs, and a high first gear meant it had to be screamed to pull away. Early imports had four speed gearboxes, but most were five speed models. The model had a pressed steel and tubular frame, and good suspension, and handled well.

The Olympique had proper footrests, but its regulation pedals, which were used for starting the engine, got in the way once the bike was under way. Other minuses were that the exhaust system made access to the centre stand difficult, the horn was puny, the speedo would have been better suited to a bicycle, and the lights and electrics were typically Italian – poor quality and unreliable.

The Malaguti Cross was a five speed dirt bike-style moped, which featured a braced duplex frame, Marzocchi hydraulic front forks, three-way adjustable hydraulic rear shock absorbers, and an alternative lower ratio rear sprocket. An engine bash plate, headlight stone guard, rubber lever covers, and a tank mounted tool pouch added to its off-road specification.

Malaguti's Super Cross, or Cavalcone, was virtually a motocross machine on the road. Large, but light at 166lbs, it had a long swinging arm, which stretched the wheelbase to 51in - much longer than average for a moped - and contributed to high speed stability on or off the road. Dirt bike features included an expansion chamber exhaust, steeply raked Marzocchi Competition shock absorbers, plastic mudguards and competition plates, adjustable alloy dog leg levers with rubber covers, a rubber mounted number plate and light assembly, headlight stoneguard, and engine bash plate.

Introduced slightly later than the Cavalcone, and available with a four or five speed gearbox, the Malaguti Monte was a similar machine in an enduro style. The Hombre was a five speed trail bike with apehanger bars that was imported from February 1974 to July 1975, and the Super Quattro, first imported in December 1974, was much like the Olympique in appearance and specification.

MALAGUTI OLYMPIQUE

Engine	Franco Morini 49.93cc two-stroke
Power	6.5bhp@8500rpm
Bore and stroke	39 x 41.8mm
Carburettor	Dell 'Orto 19mm

Malaguti Olympique. Note the twin silencer exhaust system. (Courtesy Ian Arnold)

Funky Mopeds

Electrical system	6v 18w flywheel magneto
Gears	Four/five
Fuel capacity	2.5 gallons
Weight	42lbs
Wheelbase	46 inches
Tyres	2.5 x 18 front and rear
Max speed	52mph
Fuel consumption	106mpg
Price	£205.70 in July 1974
	£251.00 in April 1977
Imported	February 1974 to July 1977

Malaguti Cross (Cavalcone).

Malaguti Super Cross (Cavalcone).

MALAGUTI CROSS (CAVALCONE)

Engine	Franco Morini 49.93cc two-stroke
Power	6.5bhp@8500rpm
Bore and stroke	39 x 41.8mm
Carburettor	Dell 'Orto SHB19/19
Electrical system	6v 18w flywheel magneto
Gears	Five
Wheelbase	46 inches
Tyres	2.5 x 19 front and 3 x 17 rear
Imported	From February 1974 to July 1975
Price	Not known

MALAGUTI SUPER CROSS (CAVALCONE)

Engine	Franco Morini 49.93cc two-stroke
Power	6.5bhp@8500rpm
Bore and stroke	39 x 41.8mm
Carburettor	Dell 'Orto SHB 19/19
Electrical system	6v 18w flywheel magneto
Gears	Five
Weight	159lbs
Wheelbase	51 inches
Tyres	2.5 x 21 front and 3 x 18 rear
Max speed	50mph
Price	£339.00 in July 1976
	£369.00 in July 1977
Imported	From January 1975 to August 1977

MALAGUTI MONTE

Engine	Franco Morini 49.93cc two-stroke
Power	6.5bhp@8500rpm
Bore and stroke	39 x 41.8mm
Carburettor	Dell 'Orto SHB 19/19

Malaguti Monte.

1970s sports mopeds

French giant, Motobecane, failed to make an impact on the UK sports moped scene.

Funky Mopeds

Mobylette Sports Speciale.

Electrical system	6v 18w flywheel magneto
Gears	Four
Weight	159lbs
Wheelbase	51 inches
Tyres	2.5 x 21 front and 3 x 18 rear
Price	£339.00 in July 1977
Imported	From September 1975 to August 1977

MOTOBECANE

The giant Motobecane concern, with factories in Saint Quentin and Patin, and across France, built its first motorcycle in 1923, and produced the Mobylette range of pressed steel frame mopeds from 1949.

The company's top of the range Sports 50 MkII was first sold in the UK in 1970. It offered reasonable performance, and looked almost like a motorcycle, so was ideally placed to sell to sixteeners when the Peyton legislation came into effect. The machine was essentially a re-styled step-through with a motorcycle seat and petrol tank. It had no gears, which made it slow off the mark, but once it gathered momentum it could reach 35mph on the flat, and over 45mph downhill. Fuel consumption was in excess of 125mpg even when thrashed.

The model was imported until June 1975 when it was replaced by the SP94 Sports Speciale.

NEGRINI

Fabbrica Ciclomotori di Mauro Negrini was established in Modena, Italy in 1934.

The Negrini Super Sprint was available in four or five speed versions, and was sold in the UK between April 1975 and January 1977. The Fuoristrada Cross, which was an Easy Rider-type moped, was available from March 1976 as a shopping bike, and from November 1976 as a sports moped. Both used the firm's own engines.

NVT

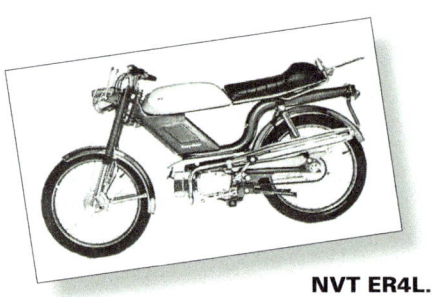

NVT ER4L.

Launched in spring 1976, the strange ER4L sixteener was a belated attempt by NVT to get in on the sixteener market. It was priced to undercut the market-leading Japanese opposition, but didn't capture the imagination of the nation's sixteen-year-olds. The ER4L had a sports seat, and dummy fuel tank to make it look more like a motorcycle, but its performance was barely better than the single and two speed automatic step-throughs in the NVT Easy Rider range, sharing its frame and many cycle parts.

Despite the fact that the three men behind the NVT ER4L were among the great names of the British motorcycle industry, the project was not a success. Doug Hele, who had been involved in BSA/Triumph racing teams, designed the frame and steering geometry, Velocette man Bertie Goodman bought in the mostly foreign component parts, and NVT's chief designer Bob Trigg was responsible for its styling.

The bike had a Franco Morini engine, and a tough tubular frame was used to contain the fuel, which it sipped at between 140 and 200mpg, depending on how hard it was ridden. It had four well spaced gears controlled by a foot shifter, a perspex screen, and a luggage rack.

NVT ER4L

Engine	Franco Morini
Gears	Four
Fuel capacity	0.75 gallons
Weight	115lbs dry
Wheelbase	45.5 inches
Max speed	40mph
Price	£215.00 in April 1977
	£237.00 in July 1977

PUCH

1970s sports mopeds

Johann Puch was a bicycle manufacturer, who built his first motorcycles at around the turn of century, although his company, Steyr-Daimler Puch, can trace its origins back to armament production in 1864.

Known colloquially in Britain as the Banana Boat or the Yellow Peril, the pressed steel famed Puch VS50 was imported from April 1972, and was one of the first attempts by a motorcycle manufacturer to provide a genuine sports moped for the British market. It sold well initially, and was described by *Motorcycle Mechanics* that year as *"...probably the nearest machine to a motorcycle that any 16-year-old enthusiast can legally ride on the roads."* but Puch's design was soon bettered by the Japanese and Italian opposition.

The VS50 used Puch's own engine with a three speed gearbox controlled by a left hand clutch twistgrip gear change. Its pedals acted as a forward rotating kickstart, and a back pedal rear brake was reasonably efficient. A conventional right hand twistgrip controlled the throttle. Top speed was over 35mph, and acceleration was reasonable; the bike looked smart with good paint finish and lots of chrome. However, the front brake was poor, and, it had crude electrics with direct lighting, a puny buzzer instead of a horn, and no ignition switch. A kill button had to be used to stop the motor. The VS50 was replaced in the Puch range by the VF50 Sport, and the company developed a series of more focused sixteener specials, starting with the M50 Sport.

Introduced to the UK in September 1973, the cherry red Puch M50 Sport was a substantial machine, and used a bolted together full cradle tubular frame derived from a larger German market model, the Jet 75. Its four speed engine was Puch's own and produced 4.25bhp@8000rpm. The bike had three position adjustable rear shock absorbers, handled well, and had a maximum speed of around 46mph. The wide gear ratios meant that the engine needed to be revved hard in every gear to maintain acceleration, especially uphill, and the gearbox was a bit clunky in operation.

The M50's pedals were used as kickstarters, and pivoted disconcertingly during riding. It had badly positioned and designed switches, and a six-volt direct ignition electrical system with no stoplight, but its brakes were reasonable, and it would return nearly 90mpg even when thrashed. Its huge petrol cap and speedometer were memorable features.

The Puch Grand Prix answered criticisms that the MS50S was overweight and underpowered. It was also cheaper. Smarter and smaller than its predecessor, the Grand Prix was a completely new model featuring a pressed steel beam frame, and FS1-E-type styling. A modified version of the four speed engine in the MS50S was tuned to produce 5.2bhp@7400rpm, and give good mid-range performance. It produced peak power at 5000rpm, and propelled the bike to a maximum of 48mph, but its one down, three up gear change remained imprecise. The Grand Prix had a slim 1.4 gallon metallic bronze petrol tank, a separate kickstart, locking pedals, which provided firm footrests, excellent brakes, and good quality Magura levers with cable adjusters.

A more expensive version of the Grand Prix, the Grand Prix Special, had a front disc brake and a black and gold paint job in the style of the JPS Lotus Formula One cars of the time. The bike had a quality air but its decals soon became tatty and its alloy finishes corroded easily. The handling, like the Grand Prix, was excellent but it had the same notchy gear change and had to be thrashed to maintain acceleration because of its wide gear ratios. Fuel consumption was reported as 150mpg ridden gently and 95mpg ridden hard. The front disc brake lacked feel but performed well even in the wet, and the narrow headlight beam was bright as long as the engine revs were kept high.

Funky Mopeds

Puch VF50, left, is similar to, and a replacement for, one of the first sports mopeds, the VS50 Sport.

Puch M50 Sport.

Puch Grand Prix.

1970s sports mopeds

Puch Grand Prix Supreme. (Artist Matt Chambers)

The Puch Grand Prix Supreme was more expensive again, and had alloy wheels. The bike continued in restricted form after August 1977 as the Monza.

PUCH VS50
Engine	Puch two-stroke
Gears	Three
Max speed	38mph
Price	£155.99 in August 1972

PUCH M50 SPORT
Engine	Puch two-stroke
Power	4.25bhp@8000rpm
Carburettor	Bing 17mm
Gears	Four
Electrical system	6v flywheel magneto
Fuel capacity	2.2 gallons
Weight	178lbs
Wheelbase	48.8 inches
Tyres	2.75 x 17 front, 3 x 17 rear
Max speed	46mph
Price	£220.00 in February 1974

Puch Grand Prix Special.

Funky Mopeds

£265.00 in March 1975

PUCH GRAND PRIX
Engine	Puch two-stroke
Power	5.2bhp@7400rpm
Carburettor	Bing 17mm
Electrical system	6v flywheel magneto
Gears	Four
Fuel capacity	1.4 gallons
Weight	158lbs
Wheelbase	47.4 inches
Tyres	2.75 x 17 front and rear
Max speed	48mph
Price	£249.00 in September 1975

PUCH GRAND PRIX SPECIAL
Engine	Puch two-stroke
Power	5.2bhp@7400rpm
Carburettor	Bing 17mm
Electrical system	6v flywheel magneto
Gears	Four
Fuel capacity	1.4 gallons
Weight	149lbs
Wheelbase	47.4 inches
Tyres	2.75 x 17 front and rear
Max speed	48mph
Fuel consumption	108mpg
Price	£326.00 in summer 1977

PUCH GRAND PRIX SUPREME
As Grand Prix Special but £30 extra (£356.00) for alloy wheels

Puch importation dates
M50 DeLuxe	From January 1973
VZ50/3P Sports	From January 1973 to January 1974
V50 Sports	From Jan to December 1974
Monza 4C	From December 1977 (restricted)

SUZUKI

East German MZ racer and two-stroke engineer, Ernst Degner, defected to the West at the Swedish Grand Prix in 1961, and spent the winter of 1961/62 working with Suzuki in Japan. As a result, the Japanese factory won the 50cc World Championship in 1962 with a disc valve induction two-stroke single. More small capacity two-stroke success followed, and Suzuki dominated 50cc world championship racing in the 1960s.

The Suzuki AP50 was very similar to the established market leader, the Yamaha FS1-E, but it was late on the scene, arriving in the UK in September 1975. Like the Yamaha, the disc valve Suzuki was a modified version of a model sold in other markets. It had a five speed gearbox, and was a bit quicker and torquier than the fizzy.

The AP50 used Suzuki's CCI lubrication system. Two-stroke oil was stored in a separate oil tank, and pressure fed to moving parts rather than mixed with petrol in the fuel tank. The bike was easy to ride, but soft suspension with bouncy springs and a complete lack of damping caused pitching, but didn't affect roadholding. AP50s were reliable with good

The Suzuki AP50 was introduced in 1975.

1970s sports mopeds

Suzuki AP50.

brakes and electrics.

SUZUKI AP50

Engine	Rotary valve two-stroke
Power	4.8bhp @ 8500rpm
Carburettor	16mm Mikuni
Electrical system	6v generator
Gears	Five
Fuel capacity	1.6 gallons
Weight	165lbs (dry)
Wheelbase	47.2 inches
Tyres	2.25 x 17 front and rear
Max speed	48mph
Price	£269.50 in April 1977

The AP50 used Suzuki's CCI lubrication system. Two-stroke oil was stored in a separate oil tank rather than mixed with the fuel.

Funky Mopeds

Testi Champion (1974).

Testi Champion (1977).

TESTI

Testis were distributed in the UK by AJW Motorcycles of Wimborne in Dorset.

The lightweight and sporty looking Testi Champion used the ubiquitous iron barrelled Minarelli moped engine with either four or six speed gearboxes. Easy to start, the Champion accelerated briskly to a top speed of over 50mph, and the reliable, rubber mounted Minarelli close ratio boxes were good for headwinds and gradients.

The double-sided, single leading shoe front brake performed adequately (the deluxe model had a hydraulic front disc), and the direct lighting and electrics were reasonable, but the suspension was undamped, causing bouncy and skittish handling, and the bike's finish was poor.

TESTI CHAMPION

Engine	Minarelli two-stroke
Power	6bhp@9000rpm
Carburettor	19mm Dell 'Orto
Electrical system	6v flywheel magneto
Gears	Six
Fuel capacity	2.6 gallons
Weight	139lbs
Wheelbase	47.75 inches
Tyres	2.5 x 17 front, 2.75 x 17 rear
Max speed	51mph
Fuel consumption	108mpg
Price	£241.00 in November 1974

YAMAHA

Now a giant conglomerate, Yamaha's origins can be traced back to 1887 when it was a reed organ manufacturing business.

The Yamaha Motor Company Ltd was founded in July 1955, and was the first Japanese company to use rotary disc valves in the production of motorcycles.

The FS1-E was introduced at the beginning of 1973, and, within three months, it was Yamaha's best selling bike in the UK. An old style Japanese small motorcycle, it had a pressed steel frame, a simple engine, and pedals to comply with the British learner law. Possibly the best all round sports moped, it was certainly the most popular, and gave thousands of youngsters a safe introduction to motorcycling.

Quickly developing a reputation for being unburstable, its reliable disc valve motor delivered zippy performance, briskly propelling the bike to a maximum speed of a little over 45mph. Its four gears were well spaced, and fuel economy was good. A balanced machine with oil damped forks, and non-adjustable rear shock absorbers, it was smooth and comfortable to ride with ultra light handling. Brakes were good, as were the lights and electrical system. Indicators were an extra on early machines, costing around £10.00 a set.

A disc brake model, the FS1-E DX, was introduced in late

1970s sports mopeds

Yamaha FS1-E DX.

Yamaha FS1-E.

Funky Mopeds

Yamaha TY50P.

1975, and the bike lived on in restricted form into the 1990s. There is a separate section devoted to this, the archetypal sports moped, elsewhere in the book.

The Yamaha TY50P, which first appeared on the British market in 1976, was a mini-trials bike rather than a trail machine. Anticipating the changes in learner legislation, its reed valve engine had a power output of only 2.9bhp@5500rpm, and the bike struggled to exceed 30mph. Nonetheless it was a neat, well engineered machine, and featured Yamaha's autolube oil lubrication system.

YAMAHA FS1-E
Engine   Disc valve two-stroke
Power   4.8bhp@7000rpm
Bore and stroke   40 x 39.7mm
Carburettor   16mm Mikuni
Electrical system   6v flywheel magneto
Gears   Four
Fuel capacity   1.5 gallons
Weight   154lbs
Wheelbase   46 inches
Tyres   2.25 x 17 front, 2.5 x 17 rear
Max speed   48mph
Fuel consumption   85mph
Price   £215.00 in March 1975
                    £230.00 in March 1976
FS1-E DX   £280.00 in April 1977

YAMAHA TY50P
Engine   49cc reed valve two-stroke
Power   2.9bhp@5500rpm

1970s sports mopeds

Bore and stroke	40 x 39.7mm
Carburettor	VM16SH
Electrical system	6v flywheel magneto
Gears	Five
Fuel capacity	6.0 litres
Weight	172lbs
Max speed	32mph
Price	£265.00 in January 1977
	£304.00 in July 1977

ZUNDAPP

Zundapp motorcycles were sold by quality and reputation, not cheap prices.

Zundapp, a German WWI munitions company, built its first motorcycles in the 1920s and 1930s, and established a dealer network. The firm then went on to produce 750cc flat twin sidecar outfits for the German army during the Second World War.

A Munich plant was opened soon after WWII, devoted to small capacity machines, and a number of new lightweight models were designed in the 1950s and '60s, including successful mopeds and scooters. The first KS models appeared in 1959.

Zundapps were also successful in motocross and trials in the 1970s.

ZUNDAPP KS50 SPORT

Tested by *Bike Magazine* at 52.72mph
Not imported in quantity

Mopeds = FUN!

Funky Mopeds

WHO DO YOU THINK YOU ARE, BARRY SHEENE?

How many 16-year-olds were asked that unimaginative question by a sarcastic copper, in the 1970s?

Barry Sheene was one of the greatest British road racers of modern times, and a giant figure on the British motorcycling scene in the 1970s. He raised the profile of biking, and bike racing to new heights, and was the first UK motorcycle racer to transcend the sport and become a household name.

How special was he? Since he retired in the early 1980s, no Briton has won a 500cc Grand Prix, let alone come remotely close to matching his achievement of winning back-to-back 500cc world championships in 1976 and 1977. Carl Fogarty? Sorry, superbike racing isn't in the same league.

He was versatile, too. Sheene won a 50cc Grand Prix on a Kreidler, and had a unique feel for setting up and racing all kinds of motorcycles.

As well as having fantastic talent, Barry Sheene was ahead of his time in recognising the commercial potential of motorcycle racing, and had the *nous* and intelligence, to exploit the fact. As well as being successful and tough, on the track and in business, he had an easy charm that endeared him to people from all walks of life.

Finally, he had a maverick streak, and was not afraid to speak his mind. He fought back bravely from two huge crashes that would have ended most riders' careers.

Chris Alty travelled to Oulton Park, in Cheshire, in the mid/late seventies to see Barry Sheene, and the rest of the best of British road racers, take on an American team led by Kenny Roberts, in the John Player Transatlantic road races.

"I can still remember it." said Chris. "The atmosphere, the smell, the fantastic sound. The big two-stroke racing bikes crackled like hell. I was in the paddock, and Barry Sheene was riding through the huge crowd, parting it as he went. I didn't see him until the last moment, and suddenly all I could

The one and only Barry Sheene.

see was the Donald Duck helmet and a big number seven. I was nearly run over. Actually, it would have been an honour."

"I was a massive fan of Barry Sheene." continued Chris. "He was the complete motorcycle racer. He didn't skulk off to his motorhome between races. He'd talk to the fans, and he didn't mind his Ps and Qs. Fag on, arm round a bird, he'd be speaking out about the other riders. Everything you wanted to hear ...

1970s sports mopeds

NUMBER ONE HIT SINGLES IN THE SPORTS MOPED ERA

The dates and weeks at number one do not always tally. This is because some songs dropped from the top, and returned a week, or two, later. The total number of weeks at the top of the charts is shown.

1971
11 December for 4 weeks: Benny Hill: Ernie (The Fastest Milkman In The West)

1972
8 January for 4 weeks: New Seekers: I'd Like To Teach The World To Sing
5 February for 2 weeks: T Rex: Telegram Sam
19 February for 3 weeks:. Chicory Tip: Son Of My Father
11 March for 5 weeks: Nilsson: Without You
15 April for 5 weeks: The Pipes And Drums Of The Royal Scots Dragoon Guards: Amazing Grace
20 May for 4 weeks: T Rex: Metal Guru
17 June for 2 weeks: Don McLean: Vincent
1 July for 1 week: Slade: Take Me Back 'Ome
8 July for 5 weeks: Donny Osmond: Puppy Love
12 August for 3 weeks: Alice Cooper: School's Out
2 September for 1 week: Rod Stewart: You wear It Well
9 September for 3 weeks: Slade: Mama Weer All Crazee Now
30 September for 2 weeks: David Cassidy: How Can I Be Sure
14 October for 4 weeks: Lieutenant Pigeon: Mouldy Old Dough
11 November for 2 weeks: Gilbert O'Sullivan: Claire
25 November for 4 weeks: Chuck Berry: My Ding-A-Ling
23 December for 5 weeks: Little Jimmy Osmond: Long Haired Lover From Liverpool

1973
27 January for 5 weeks: Sweet: Blockbuster
3 March for 4 weeks: Slade: Cum On Feel The Noize
31 March for 1 week: Donny Osmond: The Twelfth of Never
7 April for 2 weeks: Gilbert O'Sullivan: Get Down
21 April for 4 weeks: Dawn (featuring Tony Orlando): Tie A Yellow Ribbon Round The Old Oak Tree
19 May for 4 weeks: Wizzard: See My Baby Jive
16 June for 1 week: Suzi Quatro: Can The Can
23 June for 1 week: 10cc: Rubber Bullets
30 June for 3 weeks: Slade: Skweeze Me Pleeze Me
21 July for 1 week: Peters And Lee: Welcome Home
28 July for 4 weeks: Gary Glitter: I'm The Leader Of The Gang (I Am)
25 August for 4 weeks: Donny Osmomd: Young Love
22 September for 1 week: Wizzard: Angel Fingers
29 September for 4 weeks: Simon Park Orchestra: Eye Level
27 October for 3 weeks: David Cassidy: Daydreamer
17 November for 4 weeks: Gary Glitter: I Love You Love Me Love
15 December for 5 weeks: Slade: Merry Christmas Everybody

1974
19 January for 1 week: New Seekers: You Won't Find Another Fool Like Me
26 January for 4 weeks: Mud; Tiger Feet
23 February for 2 weeks: Suzi Quatro: Devil Gate Drive
9 March for 1 week: Alvin Stardust: Jealous Mind
16 March for 3 weeks: Paper Lace: Billy Don't Be A Hero
6 April for 4 weeks: Terry Jacks: Seasons In The Sun
4 May for 2 weeks: Abba: Waterloo
18 May for 4 weeks: Rubettes: Sugar Baby love
15 June for 1 week: Ray Stevens; The Streak
22 June for 1 week: Gary Glitter: Always Yours
29 June for 4 weeks: Charles Aznavour: She
27 July for 3 weeks: George McCrae: Rock Your Baby
17 August for 2 weeks: The 3 Degrees: When Will I See You Again
31 August for 3 weeks: The Osmonds: Love Me For A Reason
21 September for 3 weeks: Carl Douglas: Kung Fu Fighting
12 October for 1 week: John Denver: Annie's Song
19 October for 1 week: Sweet Sensation: Sad Sweet Dreamer
26 October for 3 weeks: Ken Boothe: Everything I Own
16 November for 3 weeks: David Essex: Gonna Make You A Star
7 December for 2 weeks: Barry White: You're The First, The Last, My Everything
21 December for 4 weeks: Mud: Lonely This Christmas

1975
18 January for 1 week: Status Quo: Down Down
25 January for 1 week: The Tymes: Ms Grace
1 February for 3 weeks: Pilot: January
22 February for 2 weeks: Steve Harley and Cockney Rebel: Make Me Smile (Come Up And See Me)
8 March for 2 weeks: Telly Savalas: If
22 March for 6 weeks: Bay City Rollers: Bye Bye Baby
3 May for 2 weeks: Mud: Oh Boy
17 May for 3 weeks: Tammy Wynette: Stand By Your Man
7 June for 3 weeks: Windsor Davies and Don Estelle: Whispering Grass
28 June for 2 weeks: 10cc: I'm Not In Love
12 July for 1 week: Johnny Nash: Tears On My Pillow

Funky Mopeds

19 July for 3 weeks: Bay City Rollers: Give A Little Love
9 August for 1 week: Typically Tropical: Barbados
16 August for 3 weeks: Stylistics: Can't Give you Anything (But My Love)
6 September for 4 weeks: Rod Stewart: Sailing
9 August for 1 week: Typically Tropical: Barbados
16 August for 3 weeks: Stylistics: Can't Give you Anything (But My Love)
6 September for 4 weeks: Rod Stewart: Sailing
4 October for 3 weeks: David Essex: Hold Me Close
25 October for 2 weeks: Art Garfunkel: I Only Have Eyes For You
8 November for 2 weeks: David Bowie: Space Oddity
22 November for 1 week: Billy Connolly: D.I.V.O.R.C.E.
29 November for 9 weeks: Queen: Bohemian Rhapsody

1976
31 January for 2 weeks: Abba: Mama Mia
14 February for 1 week: Slik: Forever And Ever
21 February for 2 weeks: Four Seasons: December '63
6 March for 6 weeks: Brotherhood Of Man: Save All Your Kisses For Me
8 May for 4 weeks: Abba: Fernando
5 June for 1 week: JJ Barrie: No Charge
12 June for 2 weeks: Wurzels: Combine Harvester (Brand New Key)
26 June for 3 weeks: Real Thing: You To Me Are Everything
17 July for 1 week: Demis Roussos: The Roussos Phenomenon EP (main track: Forever And Ever)
24 July for 6 weeks: Elton John and Kiki Dee: Don't Go Breaking My Heart
4 September for 6 weeks: Abba: Dancing Queen
11 October for 4 weeks: Pussycat: Mississippi
13 November for 3 weeks: Chicago: If You Leave Me Now
4 December for 3 weeks: Showaddywaddy: Under The Moon Of Love
25 December for 3 weeks: Johnny Mathis: When A Child Is Born

1977
15 January for 4 weeks: David Soul: Don't Give Up On Us
12 February for 1 week: Julie Covington: Don't Cry For Me Argentina
19 February for 3 weeks: Leo Sayer: When I Need You
12 March for 3 weeks: Manhattan Transfer: Chanson D'Amour
2 April for 5 weeks: Abba: Knowing Me Knowing You
7 May for 2 weeks: Deniece Williams: Free
21 May for 4 weeks: Rod Stewart: I Don't Want To Talk About It / First Cut Is The Deepest
18 June for 1 week: Kenny Rogers: Lucille
25 June for 1 week: Jacksons: Show You The Way To Go
2 July for 3 weeks: Hot Chocolate: So You Win Again
23 July for 4 weeks: Donna Summer: I Feel Love

20 August for 1 week: Brotherhood of Man: Angelo
27 August for 1 week: Floaters: Float On
3 September for 5 weeks: Elvis Presley: Way Down
8 October for 3 weeks: David Soul: Silver Lady
29 October for 1 week: Baccara: Yes Sir I Can Boogie
5 November for 4 weeks: Abba: The Name Of The Game
3 December for 9 weeks: Wings: Mull Of Kintyre

1978
4 February for 1 week: Up Town Top Ranking: Althia And Donna
11 February for 1 week: Brotherhood of Man: Figaro
18 February for 3 weeks: Abba: Take A Chance On Me
11 March for 4 weeks: Kate Bush: Wuthering Heights
8 April for 3 weeks: Brian and Michael: Matchstalk Men And Matchstalk Cats And Dogs
29 April for 2 weeks: Bee Gees: Night Fever:
13 May for 5 weeks: Boney M: Rivers of Babylon
17 June for 9 weeks: John Travolta and Olivia Newton John: You're The One That I Want
19 August for 5 weeks: Commodores: Three Times A Lady
23 September for 1 week: 10cc: Dreadlock Holiday
30 September for 7 weeks: John Travolta and Olivia Newton John: Summer Nights
18 November for 2 weeks: Boomtown Rats: Rat Trap
2 December for 1 week: Rod Stewart: Da Ya Think I'm Sexy
9 December for 4 weeks: Boney M: Mary's Boy Child / Oh My Lord

1979
6 January for 3 weeks: Village People: YMCA
27 January for 1 week: Ian Dury And The Blockheads: Hit Me With Your Rhythm Stick
3 February for 4 weeks: Blondie: Heart Of Glass
3 March for 2 weeks: Bee Gees: Tragedy
17 march for 4 weeks: Gloria Gaynor: I Will Survive
14 April for 6 weeks: Art Garfunkel: Bright Eyes
26 May for 3 weeks: Blondie: Sunday Girl
16 June for 2 weeks: Anita Ward: Ring My Bell
30 June for 4 weeks: Tubeway Army (Gary Numan): Are 'Friends' Electric
28 July for 4 weeks: Boomtown Rats: I Don't Like Mondays
25 August for 4 weeks: Cliff Richard: We Don't Talk Anymore
22 September for 1 week: Gary Numan: Cars
29 September for 3 weeks: Police: Message In A Bottle
20 October for 1 week: Buggles: Video Killed The Radio Star
27 October for 3 weeks: Lena Martell: One Day At A Time
17 November for 3 weeks: Dr Hook: When You're In Love With A Beautiful Woman
8 December for 1 week: Police: Walking On The Moon
15 December for 5 weeks: Pink Floyd: Another Brick In The Wall

1980

1970s sports mopeds

19 January for 2 weeks: Pretenders: Brass In Pocket
2 February for 2 weeks: The Specials AKA (Specials): The Specials Live EP (main track: Too Much Too Young)
16 February for 2 weeks: Kenny Rogers: Coward Of The County
1 March for 2 weeks: Blondie: Atomic
15 March for 1 week: Fern Kinney: Together We Are Beautiful
22 March for 3 weeks: The Jam: Going Underground
12 April for 2 weeks: Detroit Spinners: Working My Way Back To You
26 April for 1 week: Blondie: Call Me
3 May for 2 weeks: Dexy's Midnight Runners: Geno
17 May for 2 weeks: Johnny Logan: What's Another Year
31 May for 3 weeks: Mash: Suicide Is Painless (Theme From M*A*S*H)
21 June for 3 weeks: Don McLean: Crying
12 July for 2 weeks: Olivia Newton John and ELO: Xanadu
26 July for 2 weeks: Odyssey: Use It Up And Wear It Out
9 August for 2 weeks: Abba: The Winner Takes It All
23 August for 2 weeks: David Bowie: Ashes To Ashes
6 September for 1 week: The Jam: Start
13 September for 2 weeks: Kelly Marie: Feel's Like I'm In Love
27 September for 4 weeks: Police: Don't Stand So Close To Me
25 October for 3 weeks: Barbra Streisand: Woman In Love
15 November for 2 weeks: Blondie: The Tide Is High
29 November for 3 weeks: Abba: Super Trouper
20 December for 1 week: John Lennon: (Just Like) Starting Over
27 December for 2 weeks: St Winifred's School Choir: There's No-one Quite Like Grandma

500cc WORLD ROAD RACING CHAMPIONS

1971 Giacomo Agostini (MV Agusta)
1972 Giacomo Agostini (MV Agusta)
1973 Phil Read (MV Agusta)
1974 Phil Read (MV Agusta)
1975 Giacomo Agostini (Yamaha)
1976 Barry Sheene (Suzuki)
1977 Barry Sheene (Suzuki)
1978 Kenny Roberts (Yamaha)
1979 Kenny Roberts (Yamaha)
1980 Kenny Roberts (Yamaha)

www.veloce.co.uk
Details of all Veloce books • New book news • Special offers • Newsletter

Funky Mopeds

THAT WAS THE YEAR THAT WAS ...

1971
Green Cross Code introduced
Zig zag markings at zebra crossings
Stanley Kubrick's *A Clockwork Orange* released
Decimal coinage introduced
East Pakistan becomes the Independent Republic of Bangladesh

1972
16-year-olds restricted to riding mopeds with a maximum capacity of 50cc
Graveley Hill Interchange (Spaghetti Junction) opens
Idi Amin orders expulsion of Ugandan Asians
Mark Spitz wins seven Olympic gold medals
Three day week for industry imposed in UK during miners' strike
British direct rule imposed on Northern Ireland

1973
A temporary 50mph speed limit introduced to reduce fuel consumption due to Arab states cutting off oil supplies during the Israel – Egypt war
VASCAR (Visual Average Speed Computer and Recorder) speed detection equipment used for the first time by Essex and Southend Joint Constabulary
Reflective number plates made compulsory
Computerised driving licences issued
Multi-toned car horns banned
VAT starts April 1973 at 10 per cent
1 June, crash helmets become compulsory
Famine in Ethiopia
Sydney Opera House completed
GB, Ireland, and Denmark join EEC

1974
New vehicles licenced centrally at the Driver and Vehicle Licencing Centre at Swansea. New-style registration documents replace the existing log books.
UK inflation hits 20 per cent
World shortage causes oil prices to quadruple
Two general elections
Labour minority government
Labour wins overall majority

1975
Front number plates on motorcycles abolished on 31 July
Motorcycle MoT fee increased to £1.19 (cars £2.04)
Vietnam war ends
Spanish monarchy restored after the death of Franco
IRA holds out for six days in Balcombe Street siege
Dutch Elm disease devastates trees across the UK
Domestic video cassette recorders introduced
41 killed in Moorgate tube crash
Moped road tax was £2.50 a year
Death Race 2000 released

1976
Mini roundabouts introduced
Summer petrol prices 79p a gallon
Summer drought

1977
Mopeds redefined. New legislation comes into effect on 1 August
God Save The Queen by the Sex Pistols reaches number two (actually number one) in May
Ford launches the Fiesta
Saturday Night Fever released

1978
New edition of the *Highway Code* is published
60mph national speed limit, and 70mph motorway speed limit made permanent

1979
Tories win General Election on 4 May making Margaret Thatcher Britain's first woman Prime Minister

1980
First compact disc players released by Phillips
John Lennon and JR shot

Also from Veloce Publishing ...

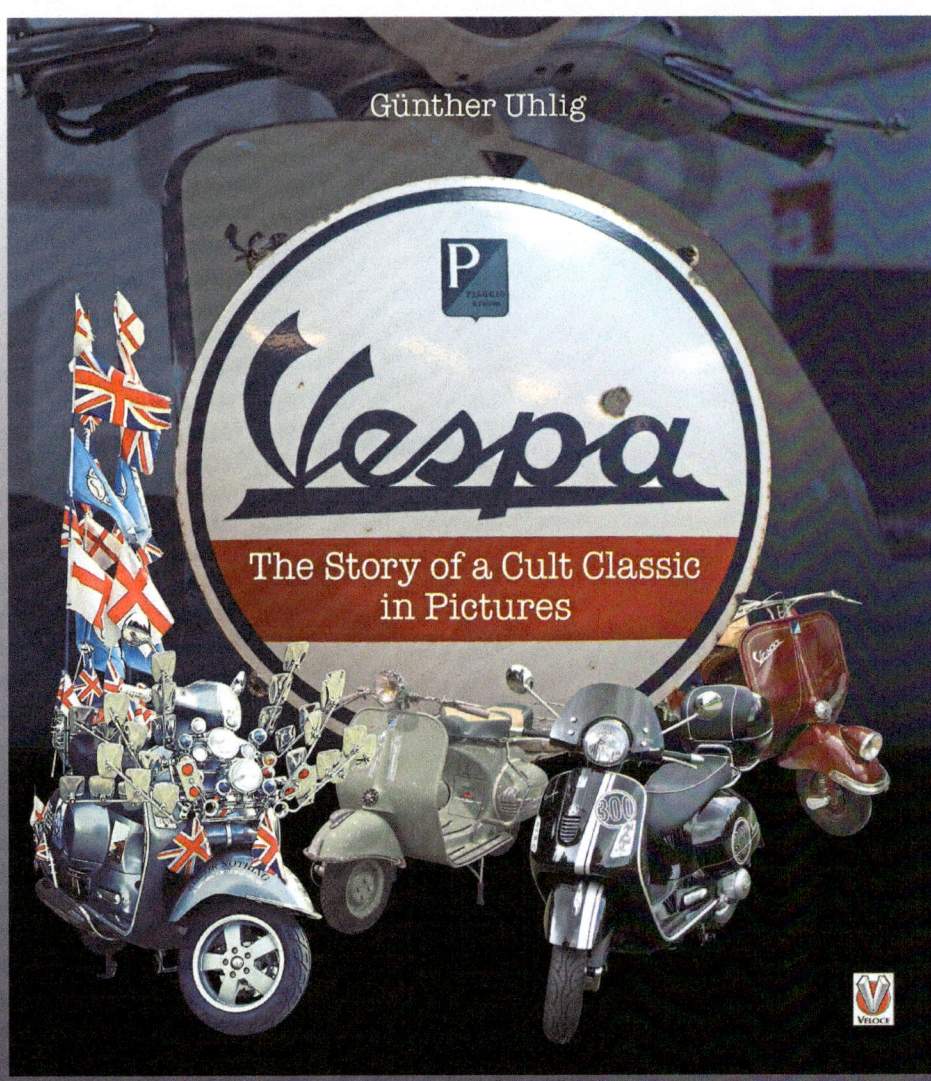

Eighteen million Vespas have buzzed their way into the world since 1946. Stood end to end, they would form a line measuring 32,000 kilometres – 20,000 miles – in length. This is an almost inconceivable statistic, as with many things that transcend conventional measures, and at some point achieve cult status. This book tells the Vespa's story and lets the reader become immersed in the culture of Vespa and la bella vita.

ISBN: 978-1-845847-90-6
Hardback • 26.5x23cm • £35* UK/$60.00* USA • 252 pages • 475 pictures

For more info on Veloce titles, visit our website at www.veloce.co.uk
email: info@veloce.co.uk • Tel: +44(0)1305 260068
* prices subject to change, p&p extra

Also from Veloce Publishing ...

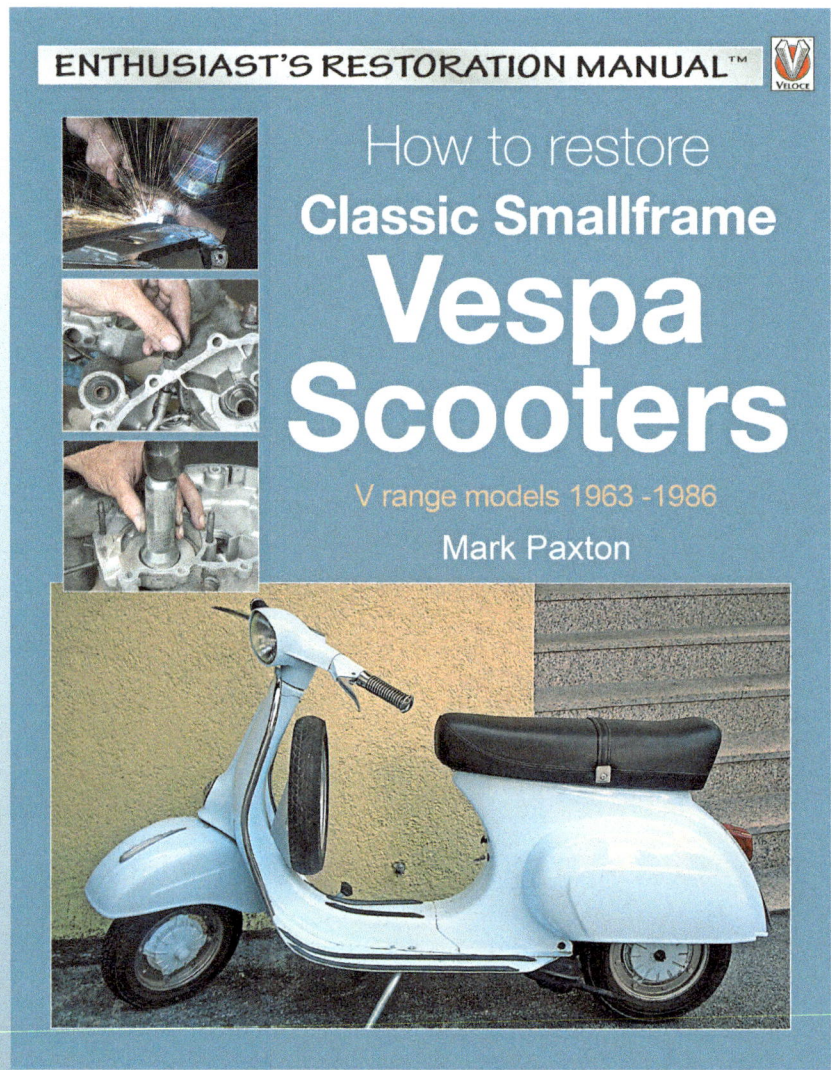

Investigates in detail the reality of small frame Vespa restoration. Aimed at the do-it-yourself enthusiast and featuring over 80 clear colour photographs, here is an essential step-by-step-guide to the complete renovation of your beloved scooter.

ISBN: 978-1-845844-37-0
Paperback • 27x20.7cm • £19.99* UK/$39.95* USA • 120 pages • 688 colour and b&w pictures

For more info on Veloce titles, visit our website at www.veloce.co.uk
email: info@veloce.co.uk • Tel: +44(0)1305 260068
* prices subject to change, p&p extra

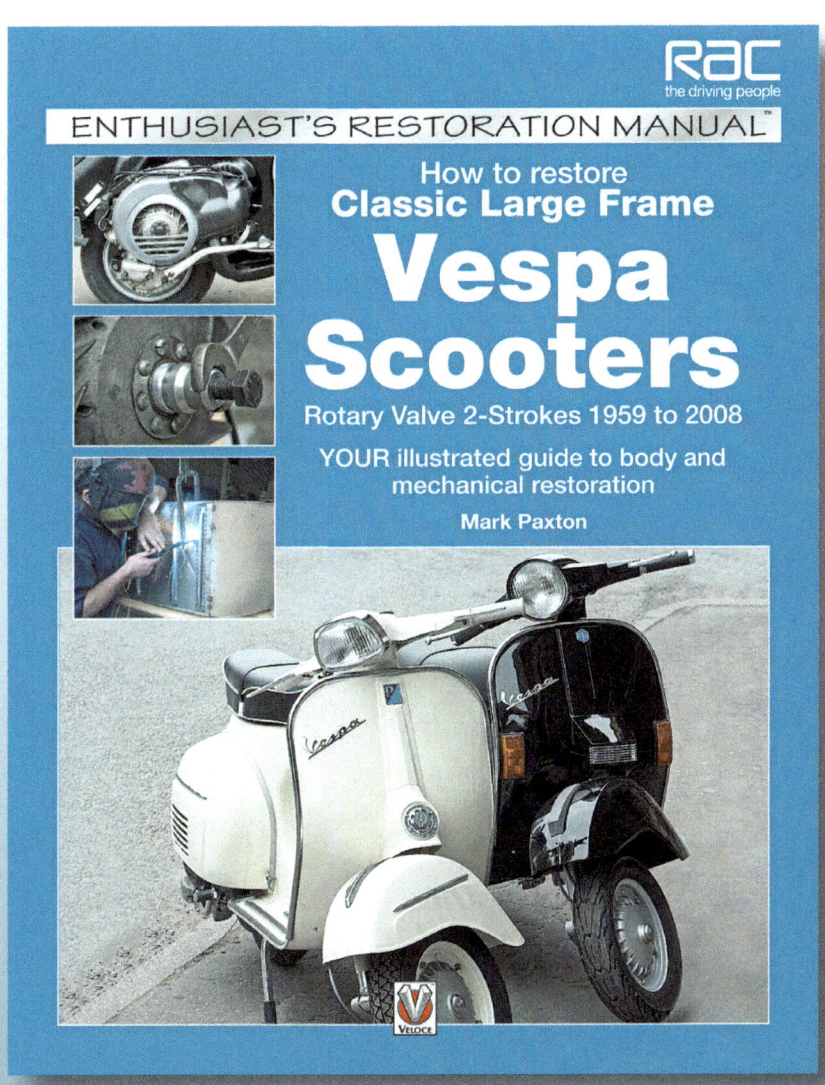

Investigates in detail the reality of Vespa restoration. Aimed at the do-it-yourself enthusiast and featuring over 875 clear colour photographs, this is an essential step-by step-guide to the complete renovation of your beloved scooter.

ISBN: 978-1-845843-24-3
Paperback • 27x20.7cm • £24.99* UK/$49.95* USA • 160 pages • 878 colour and b&w pictures

For more info on Veloce titles, visit our website at www.veloce.co.uk
email: info@veloce.co.uk • Tel: +44(0)1305 260068
* prices subject to change, p&p extra

Available from Veloce Digital ...

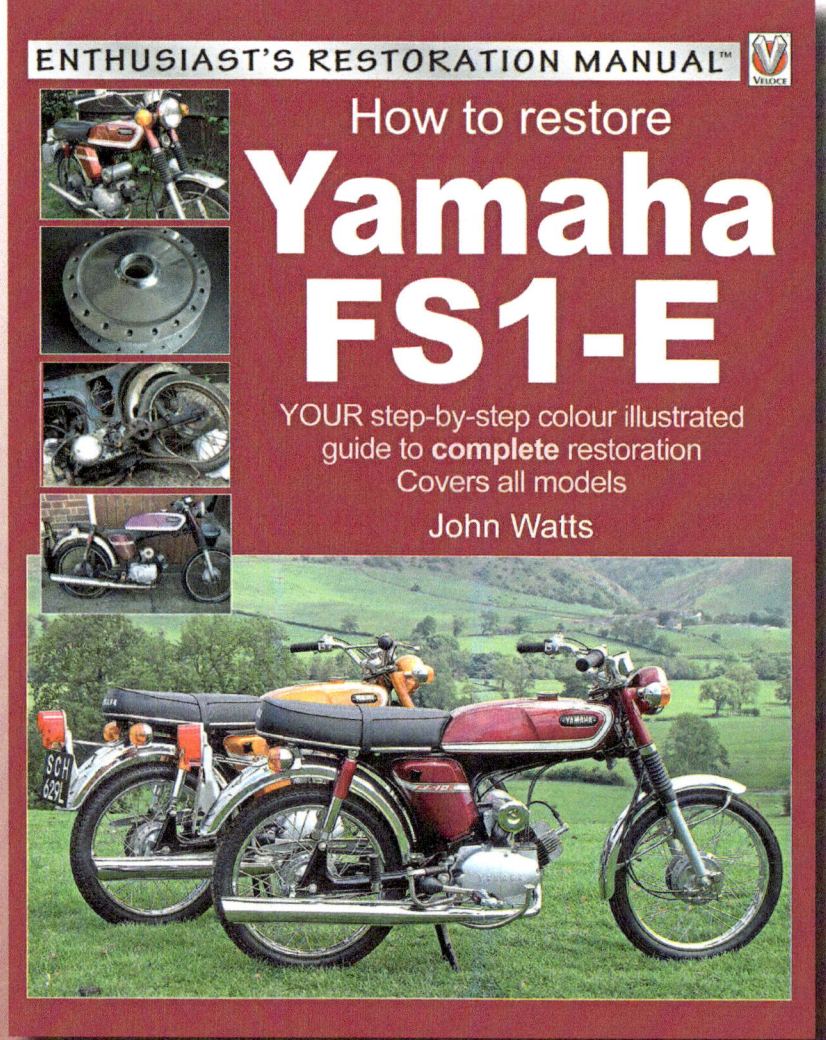

Most FS1-Es have not stood the test of time well, and very few good original examples exist. However, there are plenty of restorable machines around, and this book guides the do-it-yourself restorer through the minefield of finding a machine to restore, and the pitfalls of a first restoration.

eV4672 • Flowing layout • 225 pictures • Base price £14.99
ISBN: 978-1-845846-72-5 • UPC: 6-36847-04672-9

For more info on Veloce Digital titles, visit our website at www.digital.veloce.co.uk
email: info@veloce.co.uk • Tel: +44(0)1305 260068
* prices subject to change, p&p extra

INDEX

AA *Drive* magazine 13
Accident statistics 13, 15
Alty, Chris 18
AJW 100
AJW Greyhound 100, 101
AJW Wolfhound 100, 101

Batavus 101
Batavus Bronco 102
Batavus HS50 101, 102
Batavus MK45 101, 102
BBC Nationwide 13
Big Bore kits 65
Bike Magazine 13, 88

Casal 33, 102
Casal Phantom 5 103
Casal S2 103
Casal SS4 103
Casal ST50 Cross 103
Cimatti 103
Cimatti Bobcat 105
Cimatti Kaiman 104
Cimatti Sagittario 104
Classic Motorcycle Mechanics magazine 19, 23, 61, 62
Collecting 49, 61
Costs 30
Croxon, Gerry 19

Derbi 105
Derbi Cross 105
Derbi GT4 105
Derestricting slopeds 97
Dullens, Henk 88
Dunn, John 19

eBay 94
Electrical systems 41

Fantic Caballero 105, 106, 109
Fantic Chopper 105, 106, 109
Fantic GT 106, 109

Fantic GT Super 6 105, 106, 109
Fantic Motor 32, 41, 43, 45, 105
Fantic Super T 106, 109
Fantic T I 105, 106
Fashion 45
Fielder, Brent 17
Finding bikes and parts 52-59
Fitzsimmons, Steve 25, 39
Fizzy Galore 25, 30, 93, 94
Flandria 109
Flandria 547L 111
Flandria 547M 111
Fowlers of Bristol 88
fs1e.co.uk 25, 95

Garelli 31, 40, 41, 43, 58, 110
Garelli Rekord 10, 111, 113
Garelli Rekord Cross 111
Garelli Tiger Cross 10, 41, 111, 113
Garelli Tiger Special 114
Gilera 32, 39, 41, 43, 45, 56, 114
Gilera Enduro 114, 115
Gilera Touring 114
Gilera Trail 114, 115
Gitane 34, 40, 115
Gitane Champion 115
Gitane Champion Veloce 115
Gitane Grand Sport 117
Gitane Trail King 117
Guardian, The 14

Harglo Ltd 101, 102
Hire purchase 30, 31
Holland, Neil 21
Honda 117
Honda SS50 43, 58, 117, 118
Honda SS50 Z B2 117, 118

Insurance (PAD policies) 30

Kowaleski, Julian 21
Kreidler 118

143

Funky Mopeds

Kreidler Super Sports Deluxe 119
KTM 119-121

Legislation, 125cc limit 15
Legislation, 1971 5, 8, 28
Legislation, 1977 5, 13-15, 96

Mahon, Chris 18
Maintenance 42
Making parts 56
Malaguti 59, 81, 121
Malaguti Cross 121, 122
Malaguti Hombre 121
Malaguti Monte 121, 122
Malaguti Olympique 121
Malaguti Super Cross 121, 122
Marsden Russell & Margaret 25
Ministry of Transport 8, 12
Moore, Barry 16
Moped, definition 9
Moped, history of 9
Moped registrations 14, 28
Motobecane 124
Motorcycle Mechanics magazine 10, 14, 96, 106
Motorcycle News 26
Motorcycle registrations 13, 28
Music 62, 135

Negrini 124
Nostalgia 47
NVT 124
NVT ER4L 124

Owens, Charlie 17

Pack riding 35
Padgett, Peter 24
Padgett's of Batley 24, 90
Partners 59
Pedals & pedalling 43
Performance kits 14
Performance restrictions 96
Peyton, John 5, 8, 10
Piaggio 114
Police 39
Powell, John 20
Prices 31
Puch 33, 124

Puch Grand Prix 126, 128
Puch Maxi 9
Puch M50 Sport 125, 127
Puch VF50 Sport 125
Puch VS50 10, 125, 127

Raleigh Chopper 48, 63
Reliability 42
Restoration skills 59
Restoring 49-52, 58, 67-69

Sears, Russell 25
Sheene, Barry 118, 134
Sherburn Milk Bar 49
Silvester, Terry 27
Simcox, Paul 23
Slopeds 14, 96
SMOC 18-23, 48, 49, 61
SMOC runs 63
Speed 37, 39
Stafford classic motorcycle shows 22, 23, 25
Stillgoe, Richard 14
Storage 61
Stupidity 37
Sunrise graphics 52
Suzuki 82, 128
Suzuki AP50 128, 129

Testi 129, 130
Training & tests 34, 45
Transport & Road Research Laboratory 15
Tuning 15

Used Bike Guide magazine 23

Wilkinson, Steve 26
Wilson, Mark 20
Wright (Bob Wright Motorcycles) 56

Yamaha 130
Yamaha DT50 97
Yamaha F5B 88
Yamaha FS1 88
Yamaha FS1E 10, 28-32, 41, 43, 56, 88-94
Yamaha RD50 99
Yamaha TY50P 132

Zundapp 133

Printed and bound by CPI Group (UK) Ltd, Croydon, CR0 4YY
22/03/2026
02076055-0014